A Concise Survey of

German Literature

H. B. GARLAND

Emeritus Professor of German
University of Exeter

First edition 1971
Second edition 1976

Published by
THE MACMILLAN PRESS LTD
London and Basingstoke
Associated companies in New York
Dublin Melbourne Johannesburg and Madras

ISBN 0 333 21362 9 (hardcover)
ISBN 0 333 21363 7 (paperback)

Printed in Great Britain by
RICHARD CLAY (THE CHAUCER PRESS), LTD
Bungay, Suffolk

Contents

Preface to the First Edition

Nowadays excellent composite works by groups of specialists cater for the needs of the advanced reader and for constant reference. Short works giving a quick preliminary orientation hardly exist. Yet a quick survey which can be read, say, in two evenings is something which both the general reader and the new student need as a starting-point. Some sixty years ago J. G. Robertson followed up his large and detailed *History of German Literature* with a highly readable account in the Home University Library, and a generation later G. Waterhouse did it again in the Benn's Sixpenny series. The need persists, as I know from long experience and the present book is intended to meet it once more. My aim is to give in readable form and modest dimensions a survey of German literature from the beginnings to the present day which will provide a kind of scale map of names, a quick means of orientation on the salient points in a large territory. It does not encroach on any of the larger treatises for more advanced readers. Indeed it may be regarded as an introduction to them, and in order that it may the better fulfil that purpose, it is provided with a brief appendix listing some easily accessible larger works which are equipped with good bibliographies. It is, however, complete in itself, and the casual inquirer will read it, I hope, with some profit even if he intends to go no further.

An account such as this is necessarily selective, and nowhere more so than when it reaches the German literature of our own age. At one time historians of literature not infrequently solved this problem by omitting contemporary writing altogether. Such a restriction is clearly no longer possible in our own exceptionally self-conscious age; on the other hand, on such a small scale as this book, anything approaching comprehensiveness in treating present-day writing is not feasible either, and so names must be omitted which some would wish to see included, and no two persons are likely to agree at all points on which authors should be in and which out.

In such a short survey it seems essential that the historical background should not be overlooked and accordingly reference is made from time to time to points of political, social and economic history in order to give coherence to a large canvas peopled by separate figures more remarkable for their individual than for their generic characteristics.

German literature has a wide geographical spread, and for this reason a map is included.

H.B.G.

Preface to the Second Edition

The success of the first edition has encouraged me in this second edition to expand the final chapter, and especially the last section 'The Second World War and After', providing more information and bringing it right up to date.

H.B.G.

June 1976

1 The Earliest German Literature: 700–1000

It is not easy to know where to begin. With the Germanic peoples and their songs, as Tacitus described them in A.D. 98? Or with the lays – lost because they were not written down – sung by their descendants crossing and re-crossing Europe in the centuries of migration which weakened and extinguished the Roman Empire? Certainly German historians of literature, out to demonstrate that German civilisation was as old and venerable as the *imperium romanum* and the Christian Church, used to feel bound to set themselves such tasks of hypothetical reconstruction. Now that nationalism in literary history has been discredited, and since this is anyway a book in English for English-speaking readers, we can excuse ourselves from such gropings in darkness, and begin at the point when written scraps survive in a language which, though strange to us, is clearly a kind of German.

It was about the end of the eighth century that the word *deutsch* began to be applied to the language spoken by the eastern Franks, a language which has since come to be called Old High German. And it is perhaps an unintentional comment on the worth of the surviving literature, that it used to be customary to speak of 'Old High German Literature', using a linguistic term to delimit a period of letters. Comment or not, it seems better to abandon this philological description and to speak instead of 'the earliest German literature', all the more so since one of the important poems is not Old High but Old Low German or, as it is otherwise called, Old Saxon. Under that heading can reasonably be included the literary remains of the eighth, ninth and tenth centuries.

It is a long period and it has a meagre crop of literary documents. The remnants of this literature, which can never have been abundant, are rarely creative or poetic, at any rate before the ninth century. Most of them are legal or liturgical or theological translations, which in a more prolific period would have been discarded. But if they are not examples of poetic art, they are at least fragments of history, scraps from men's lives. They originated in a great kingdom, the Frankish Empire, which reached a first peak under Charles the Great, crowned Emperor in 800. It was a land which covered present-day France, Switzerland, the Low Countries and Germany roughly up to the Elbe. It was a realm and an age of action. The peasants, the warriors, the rulers themselves could not read or write. The Empire needed a machinery of administration, and all its clerical work was truly 'clerical', for the clergy was the only class capable of performing it. The language of the Church, however, was Latin, and so the sparseness of German documents is the more readily comprehensible. Moreover the records which have survived, German or Latin, have had to escape the dangers of fire, flood and neglect, as well as deliberate destruction in many ages when men saw no point in preserving what was not immediately useful. It is perhaps surprising that anything has survived the intervening thousand years.

The oldest of the literary remains of these early centuries are two short poems. They were not intended as art but as practical poetry, with a purpose; for they are magic spells for incantation, the one to secure the escape of a prisoner, the other to cure a lame horse. Many other magic spells are known, some perhaps in origin as ancient, but all the rest have been christianised. Only these two, known as the *Merseburger Zaubersprüche*, because they were written (perhaps by a superstitious monk) on a blank page of a tenth-century MS. found in Merseburg Abbey, invoke ancient Germanic gods and are handed down intact from pre-Christian days.

Though the functional *Merseburger Zaubersprüche*, with their stark rhythm and alliterative pattern, impress as poetry, they are greatly surpassed by a heroic lay, surviving almost complete and almost miraculously. It is clearly descended from the lost oral bardic poetry. The *Hildebrandslied* tells a story common to many early peoples, found in Persia in the story of Sohrab and Rustum and in Ireland in that of Cuchullain. The great warrior Hildebrand and his son Hadubrand, who are early separated, encounter each other years later as champions of two opposing armies. The father suspects the son's identity and seeks to avoid the contest, but the son will have none of this and the two do battle. No doubt Hildebrand killed Hadubrand, but the end, apparently for lack of space, is missing. The poem was written down by monks about A.D. 810 on two spare pages of a theological MS. The tragic grandeur of this alliterative poem, part of which is in dialogue, is unmistakable. We cannot know for certain how the original hearers responded, but the *Hildebrandslied* is still for us a moving work.

From somewhere between 770 and 800 there survives a partly poetic fragment known as *Das Wessobrunner Gebet*, a title referring to its discovery at Wessobrunn Abbey in Bavaria. It consists of a short passage of alliterative verse describing, with what seems to us sublime economy, the primal chaos in which God alone existed; the second part is a prayer in prose.

Though the scale of these works is not small, they are short. The earliest large-scale work is a life of Christ in the form of a heroic epic written in Old Saxon during the reign of Ludwig the Pious (814–40) and known since its discovery in 1830 as *Der Heliand*. In this substantial poem of nearly 6000 lines the Saviour (*Heliand*) is seen, in the mirror of the age, as a German prince supported by his thanes, the disciples. For all its heroic costume, a scene such as the Crucifixion is movingly portrayed and the piety of the author, no doubt a cleric, is plainly evident.

The *Heliand* is a Gospel harmony, a continuous narration that is based on a collation of the Gospels. A generation later another 'harmony' was written by the Benedictine monk Otfried of Weissenburg (Wissembourg) in Alsace. Otfried's *Evangelienbuch* is a painstaking poem, telling the Gospel story in sections, interspersed with comments of edification and devotion. If the work seems today less than adequate as poetry, that should not be held against Otfried, who saw his task as one of service and utility. He seems to have been an earnest and conscientious scholar as well as a devout Christian and he was more concerned with substance than manner. All the same, he intended his *Evangelienbuch* to supplant in great houses the profane heroic lays (such, no doubt, as the *Hildebrandslied*). Since his book exists in three complete MSS. (a remarkable number for so early a work), Otfried's poem manifestly appealed to the hearers of his age. In one important respect Otfried is a technical innovator – abandoning the alliterative structure hitherto used in verse, he made of the *Evangelienbuch* the first German rhyming poem. This example was followed in a short religious poem written about fifty years later by a monk of Reichenau which tells of Jesus meeting at the well the woman of Samaria (*Christus und die Samariterin*).

Other poetic remains are slender. A fragment of a poem in alliterative verse, conjuring up a vivid picture of the Last Day and delivered in a tone of vehement pulpit rhetoric, survives from the late ninth century. Itself untitled, it was called by its first editor *Muspilli*. The victory of Louis (Ludwig) III, King of the West Franks, over the Normans at Saucourt in 881 is celebrated in rhyming pairs in the *Ludwigslied*, a song glorifying the king, in whose battle cry 'Kyrrieleison' Church and State are united. A hymn to St George (*Georgslied*), written about 900, is so extravagant in its spelling that it can only with difficulty be deciphered; indeed it seems to have defeated the tenth-century copyist. And a handful of christianised magic spells from the ninth and tenth centuries, including a particularly charming one for a bee-keeper seeking to control his bees (*Lorscher Bienensegen*), completes the tale.

Poetry was in that age the proper vehicle for what was to elevate or to entertain; prose was unliterary and utilitarian, and the accumulation of prose documents in the eighth, ninth and tenth centuries is an odd and drab one. With so few records, of course, fragments of negligible significance achieve an unexpected prominence. Legal documents such as the *Hamelburger* and *Würzburger Markbeschreibungen* define the limits of landed property. The *Strassburger Eide* record the oaths publicly sworn in German and Romanic (*romana lingua*) by Ludwig the German and Charles the Bald at

Strasburg in 842. The *Taufgelöbnisse* preserve the formulae by which the heathen (whether converted by persuasion or the sword) made their abjuration of the works of the Devil and their confession of faith in Jesus Christ.

The most substantial prose remains, however, are translations, ranging from the Lord's Prayer in the *Freisinger Paternoster* or the *Weissenburger Katechismus*, through a version of the Benedictine *Regula*, to weighty works of theology such as Bishop Isidor's seventh-century *Contra Judaeos*, translated in the eighth or ninth century, or the second-century Gospel harmony of Tatian, rendered into German in the ninth century. For such Latin prose originals German prose was an appropriate medium. The main literary interest of all these works resides in their effort to temper an unsophisticated vernacular so as to render it capable of clear and precise expression.

At the very end of this period a great grammarian, Notker Labeo of St Gall (*c.* 950–1022), developed German prose for the first time into a flexible and subtle instrument for the exposition of thought or the description of fact.

The monks of course wrote much in Latin and from this age some notable poetic works in Latin have survived, including an epic poem, *Waltharius*, written in Virgilian hexameters, and an animal story, *Ecbasis captivi*, in which the calf, after a temporary escape into the world, finds his byre safer. The first plays written in Germany, Latin versions of legends, are the work of the tenth-century nun Hrotswith (Roswitha) of Gandersheim in Brunswick.

The world in which the early German records of poetry and prose were written, though largely illiterate, was not uncivilised. It saw the fashioning of the great empire of Charles the Great and, after a period of decline, its revival two centuries later under Otto the Great (936–73). Its virtues and vices were those of action: courage and endurance on the one side, ruthless ambition, vengefulness and treachery on the other. The lives of the common people were hard, frugal and wearisome, the lives of the nobility often cut short by violence. The regular web of life was frequently torn apart by internecine wars or the wanton slaughter and destruction wrought

15

by wide-ranging hordes of Norsemen, Hungarians or Slavs. The enduring cohesion amidst all the forces of disintegration was largely provided by the Roman tradition, and this tradition was preserved by the clergy, the only literates in the land, who used their learning and linguistic skill in the service of the State as well as the Church, and contrived in a few poetic works to add something of grace to an age of iron.

2 The Middle Ages

1. Anxiety and Reform: 1000–1150

The literature of the ninth and tenth centuries had suggested stirrings and preparation rather than achievement. Notker Labeo, who, in its most important aspect, the development of a literary language, represents its highest point, bequeathed to the next generation a flexible and expressive linguistic instrument. Yet his successors in the eleventh century could scarcely find any use to put it to. This seems the more surprising, since the first half of the century saw a great strengthening of Imperial power under Henry II and Henry III, who with Conrad II reigned from 1002 to 1056. Yet temporal power was not likely to foster literature as long as those who wielded it were illiterate. And as to the clergy, and especially the monastic clergy, who had time to write, their minds were directed away from the things of this world by a new spiritual ferment in the Church.

Outwardly the first unmistakable sign of the transformation in the Church's outlook is its dissociation from the temporal power of the Empire, reflected in the bitter struggle between Pope Gregory VII and the Emperor Henry IV culminating in the well-known submission of the Emperor at Canossa in 1077. But the turning away from mundane things and worldly leaders goes back to the turn of the century. The insecurity of life, the fear of damnation and widespread apprehension that the end of the world would follow closely on the year 1000 impelled men to look inside themselves and to listen to the saintly men who called them to a new way of life. And so there came about at the beginning of the century a vigorous movement for the reform of the monasteries, an emphasis on discipline and asceticism, a rejection of the lures and attrac-

17

tions of the world and a single-minded dedication to God, accompanied by mortification of the flesh and meditation upon death. The monasteries had so far been the nurseries of literature, but clearly this new austerity was unlikely to countenance poetry which gave pleasure, whether secular or sacred.

The climate of monastic reform was, however, not the only factor which was unpropitious to the development of literature. It was an age also of political stress, of economic and social instability. The great nobles were for ever conspiring and rising against the Emperor, the Emperor was frequently absent on the quest for power in Italy, columns of brutal marauders from the east and north ranged right into the heart of the country, and a largely idle and corrupt parish clergy failed to minister to spiritual needs. A sense of impending doom, of the imminent wrath of God, spread a deep malaise, which was broader and more pervasive than the monastic reform movement.

In the first half of the eleventh century there is virtually no literature. The interest in the profane classics fostered by Notker wilted as the focus of monastic life shifted away from letters. A single MS. of sermons translated from the Latin (*Wessobrunner Predigten*) is the meagre output of more than a generation. Though the records are less sparse in the second half of the century, they give no suggestion of a coherent live tradition. *Otlohs Gebet*, written down about 1060, is another translation, a rendering of a Latin prayer composed by a monk at St Emmeram's Abbey, Regensburg; and Williram's *Hohes Lied* is a German commentary on the Latin text of the Song of Songs. The *Annolied* is an original work of more ambitious character. It is a verse biography, epic in style, of Archbishop Anno of Cologne, who died in 1075, and it was intended as propaganda to promote Anno's canonisation. The *Ezzolied* or *Ezzos Gesang*, existing complete only in a confused version, partly from the eleventh (*c.* 1060) and partly from the twelfth century, is a declaration of the Christian faith, tracing biblical history from the Creation to Christ's assurance of salvation. A holy exaltation pervades the poem, which was probably sung in procession on a pilgrimage to the Holy Land, in which

18

Bishop Gunther of Bamberg took part in 1064–5. A few years later (about 1070) was written the first work which fully expresses the new asceticism. *Memento mori* (it is a modern title, the original has no superscription) is a powerful injunction, written in strophic verse, to remember that in the midst of life we are in death, and that according to our deserts, so we shall fare well or ill at the Last Day. This reminder of inescapable death and warning against the snares of the world was in all likelihood written by an abbot of Zwiefalten in Swabia, whose name is given as Noker.

With the coming of the twelfth century the records of literature become a shade more numerous. For the first forty or fifty years the writings are almost exclusively religious and the authors either clerics or pious men who have given their lives to God. Poetic laments of sinfulness (*Sündenklagen*) bring a new vein of expression and multiply rapidly. They are not the satirist's denunciation of the shortcomings of others but a remorseful personal confession of wrongs done, together with a prayer to God for forgiveness. Three complete (or almost complete) *Sündenklagen* survive, named after the libraries where the MSS. were discovered: they are the *Milstätter*, *Vorauer* and *Rheinauer Sündenklagen*, the first two in verse, the last (a slightly later example) in prose. To these must be added some fragments known as the *Klagenfurter Gebete*, and rhyming Confession preserved at Uppsala; while the *Rheinauer Paulus* and the *Cantilena de conversione Sancti Pauli* are closely related to the personal *Sündenklagen*, representing Paul's confession of his sinful life before his conversion. Through all these works runs the sense of doom and the urgent and vehement quest for salvation.

Other less personal and anguished poems sought to bring home to the layman the truths of religion and especially the promise of salvation. *Summa Theologiae* condenses into thirty-one verses the whole of biblical history and the doctrine of the Church, and the fragmentary *Mittelfränkische Reimbibel* retells the Bible story in verse. Both of these date from about 1125. Similar in purpose are the rhyming versions of Genesis and Exodus, the oldest of which is the *Wiener*

Genesis, written in Carinthia about 1075. The remainder (*Wiener Exodus, Milstätter Genesis* and *Exodus*) were probably written some fifty years later. The aim of permeating the life of the laity with religion is also pursued in poems treating picturesque or even sensational religious subjects, such as *Die drei Jünglinge im Feuerofen, Judith* (known as *Die ältere Judith*, because there exists another written a century later) and a poem about Tobias by Pfaffe Lamprecht. All these, which are virtually biblical ballads with a popular appeal, were written in the early part of the twelfth century. Other poems, appealing to a more sophisticated public, lay their stress less upon story-telling than upon biblical commentary, as in the Pentateuch from Vorau (*Vorauer Bücher Mosis*) and *Das himmlische Jerusalem*, which dates from 1130 to 1140. A simply and sincerely told life of Jesus in verse, written about 1125, is remarkable in being the work of a woman, Frau Ava, an anchoress, whose death is recorded for 1127 in the archives of Melk Abbey, Austria. All this literature of religious education has a generic uniformity and, with a few exceptions, an absence of personal imprint, which may seem to the modern reader characterless. But the standpoint of the time was necessarily different. These paraphrases of the Bible were tasks undertaken in the service of God, to whom the individual writer subdued him or herself. Group conformity counted more than personal assertion.

Though biblical narration and interpretation imposed upon the clerics narrow limits, there remained at least one field of religious writing where a deep personal commitment was legitimate – and that was the confession. Such a poem is the verse sermon from the decade 1150–60 by a poet calling himself 'ih arme Hartmann'. Who 'I, poor Hartmann' was is unknown and where he lived uncertain, but he seems to have been a man of rank, who gave up wealth and family in order to save his soul by repentance and mortification. His poem, called *Rede vom Glauben*, which is formally an exposition of the Nicene Creed, powerfully urges his hearers to repent likewise. The injunction of the sermon arises out of a personal experience of guilt and conversion. Even more eloquent, because the author had unusual poetic gifts, is the poem called

Von des tôdes gehugede ('Erinnerung an den Tod'), which was written about the middle of the century (1150–60) by a poet called Heinrich von Melk. Like 'poor Hartmann' he seems to have given up the world and become a lay brother in a monastery. *Von des tôdes gehugede* is the starkest expression of *memento mori*, reminding men with grisly detail that the flesh withers and decays, rejecting possessions and the lusts of the flesh, and insisting that salvation can only be found in mortification and in the ceaseless thought of one's end and of the Judgement to come. More than any other work of that age it allows a glimpse into the burning belief and sombre vision which led men to give up all their worldly goods, devoting the remainder of their lives to the worship of God and the contemplation of death.

2. The Claims of Life Renewed: 1130–1170

The stern and passionate asceticism of Heinrich von Melk and 'poor Hartmann', shared by many less articulate souls, was not the whole picture. Though an eleventh-century Emperor (Henry II) was canonised in 1146 and though he and his successors saw the Emperor as the guardian of a religious trust, the fiercest dissension had arisen in the second half of the eleventh century. Under Henry IV and Henry V a bitter series of humiliations and outrages, depositions and excommunications spread over fifty years, and the ceaseless preoccupation of the Emperors with the attractions of power in Italy left Germany and its people exposed to all manner of rapine, tyranny and exploitation, which stood in sharp relief against the saintliness of the ascetics. Only sporadically did the impulse to renunciation prevail. For the most part, territory and the power that went with extensive lands took first place. And so the worldly life, though in the literature of the Reform it was either ignored or reprobated, kept its hold upon most of the great.

In the end a religious motive took hold of and canalised the interests of the worldly. As early as 1064 the Archbishop of Mainz and the Bishop of Bamberg set out on a great, if unsuccessful, pilgrimage to the Holy Land. Towards the end of the century a new consciousness of the East arose, in which fear of Turkish expansion and religious shame that the holy places were in infidel hands were intermixed. The first crusade (1096–9) began to open men's eyes to hitherto unsuspected treasures and wonders, to laws and customs strange to Christendom. A new interest in the wonderful and the fabulous began to filter into the consciousness of those who wrote, providing a new channel of worldly literature, which the second crusade (1147–9), despite its military and political failure, augmented still further. And not only did the crusades open and enlarge horizons, they gave the mounted warrior, the knight, a religious glamour as the dedicated prosecutor of a holy war. Beside the religious current there came a new temporal trend. The kings and great nobles began to see in the skill of their poets an adornment of their courts and even a memorial of their greatness.

The long poems which then provided courtly entertainment were painstakingly put together over long periods, and sometimes that which one hand had begun was finished by another. So the first long poem on Alexander the Great, the *Alexanderlied*, was undertaken, as the opening lines tell us, by Lamprecht, a priest (Pfaffe Lamprecht). This was about 1135, and it was completed some thirty years later (*c.* 1160–70) by an unknown successor. The *Alexanderlied*, which initiates a long sequence of medieval German poems adapted from French originals, tells amidst spectacular and grandiose adventures of Alexander's meteoric rise to world dominion, of his brilliant but brief reign, cut short by his death by poison. So much glory is seen in the end to occupy but seven feet of earth; and the author carefully points the moral of *memento mori* in a final sermon. Yet Alexander, though he is a warning, is also the hero of the poem, a knight of valour and virtue. And so the ecclesiastical doctrine of the vanity of earthly things and the dawning chivalric ideal coexist in this poem; and they are joined by a new element, derived from the crusades, in the shape of the fabulous beings and sights of the Orient which Alexander encounters on his journeying. Though the work thus has some historical importance, Lamprecht was no more than a dull journeyman of a poet who was unable to bring his subject to life.

Much about the same time as the *Alexanderlied*, what is often reckoned to be the first historical work in German was begun. The *Kaiserchronik* is a catalogue of all the Emperors (including some who are imaginary), taking its start with Augustus and treating the Empire of ancient Rome and the German 'Roman' Empire of the Middle Ages as identical. It comes right up to date, closing at 1147 in the reign of Conrad III, only a short time before it is believed to have been completed. Though it is the work of monks and though the central ideal of this long poem of more than 17,000 lines is that of the Christian king, the *Kaiserchronik* is by its subject concerned with the events of the world and with temporal power, and so emphasises the secular element in the new literature.

Some fifteen years or so after these two works were started, a poem was written which was entirely worldly, having virtually no contact with religion, notwithstanding its author was a priest. *König Rother* (*c*. 1150) is a lively adventure story in some 5,000 lines of verse, the medieval equivalent of a novel. It tells of Rother's elopement with a princess from Constantinople, of her being carried back again, and of a second attempt at elopement which achieves success only after it has come desperately near to disaster. Part of its setting is in the Near East, but its interest depends, not on fabulous creatures and unimagined wonders but on dangers successfully braved, audacity rewarded and catastrophe averted by a hair's breadth – the typical ingredients, in fact, of an adventure story. It provided a new and lighter kind of entertainment for the leisure hours of great noblemen and their courts.

Only a few years later, about 1170, there was introduced into Germany a story of a nobler kind. The *Rolandslied*, a free translation of the French *Chanson de Roland* (*c*. 1100), was made by a monk named Conrad (Pfaffe Konrad) at Regensburg. The story is taken from the withdrawal of Charles the Great in 778 from his expedition to Spain and tells how the rearguard under Roland is cut off and annihilated by the Moors. Only at the last desperate moment does Roland sound the horn which, too late, recalls Charles.

Though it is set in Spain, the *Rolandslied*, which has real poetic qualities, is virtually a crusading poem, for death on the battlefield is seen as a form of martyrdom. Religion re-establishes itself in this poem, for the battle is not for temporal power but for the Kingdom of God.

Herzog Ernst, on the other hand, which was written almost at the same time as the *Rolandslied*, asserts the new form of literary entertainment as we see it in *König Rother*. Echoes of history a century or two before are discernible in it, and the hero bears the name of a figure in real life, but its true subject is the succession of fantastic adventures through which Ernst passes, including that of the magnetic mountain which attracts ships to their doom. It is these exploits which provide the entertainment, rather than the framework in which Ernst is slandered, outlawed and then, after his exotic experiences, received back into favour by the Emperor. Yet in spite of all the wonders the frame has its part to play. For it displays Ernst's great virtue of unshakeable loyalty, and the priest who wrote the poem implies his belief in a supreme Emperor and an undivided Empire.

3. The Flowering of Medieval Literature: 1170–1230

The Germans call the literature of the generations to either side of the year 1200 the *Blütezeit*, and the word is apter than some other literary terms, for the suddenness and lavishness suggest a season of bloom. The medieval poets whose names are most familiar, Walther von der Vogelweide, Wolfram von Eschenbach and Gottfried von Strassburg, wrote in this span of sixty years, and around them and beside them were a host of lesser talents. Both the abundance and the quality of the new literature contrast with what went before it. Up to the impact of the first lyric poets about 1160 and of the first narrative works of Hartmann von Aue about 1180, clumsiness and heavy-handedness make it clear that those who write do so without vocation; though their work is patient and even conscientious, they have not begun to grasp the necessity of craftsmanship and skill. They wrote for a public with undeveloped literary

24

standards, which was easily satisfied by the products of painstaking industry.

No doubt all the time a new and highly civilised society was emerging, which then unfolded and matured with great rapidity; and with it came a mental climate of sensitiveness and receptiveness, which was especially favourable to literature. The centre of this new articulate society was the order of chivalry, which now attained a sophistication new to the laity of the Middle Ages. The glorification of the idealised mounted warrior is epitomised in the brilliant Whitsun festive gathering at Mainz (*Mainzer Pfingstfest*), held in 1184 by the Emperor Frederick I (Barbarossa) for the admission of his two sons to the order of knighthood. The chivalric and the courtly coincide, for the great lords who hold court are surrounded by knights. Though the order of knighthood received ecclesiastical blessing and though the ceremony of admission was liturgical, the new society represented a shift in favour of the laity, who for the first time since the ancient bard (or *scopf*) unequivocally set the tone in literature; and this, of course, implies that the laymen received and valued educational advantages which hitherto had been the monopoly of the clergy. Moreover, in the new poetry which the knights and their companions composed, human love (*Minne*) is for the first time the theme, with a consequent rise of importance in the treatment of women in literature. A remarkable fact about this highly civilised society is the growth of a convention by which the woman, in poetry at any rate, is seen as the man's superior. The knight defers to his lady (who is usually married and inaccessible), worshipping from afar and conceding to her an educating and civilising influence upon him. This elevation of the woman had perhaps some connection with the adoration of the Virgin Mary; it is also widely considered that it represents a kind of allegory of the feudal system, in which the lady stands for the lord and the knight for her vassal. That the 'lord' should be a woman is a sure symptom of sophistication and a proof of the rapid evolution of this courtly and chivalric society.

The new literature of the late twelfth century was almost exclusively poetic, and the two forms which achieved almost equal popularity were the lyric and the epic. The epic had existed for centuries, but lyric poetry was new. The earliest recorded lyric poet was an Austrian knight, Der von Küren-berg, who wrote round about 1160. Attributed to him are fourteen stanzas of relatively warm and direct love poetry, but since several of them (including his most famous one, which sings of a falcon) appear to be set in the mouth of a woman, it is clear that these are not outpourings of personal emotion but entertainment within a convention and intended for public performance. A notable but perhaps misleading name in the early poetry is Dietmar von Aist, to whom the manu-scripts attribute a large number of stanzas, which include some exceptionally beautiful poems. But these are probably by several authors, so that tempting conclusions about Diet-mar as a poet of transition from simple love poetry to courtly *Minne* cannot rightly be drawn.

The courtly convention of love, in which the woman stands remote and unattainable, begins to emerge in poetry written towards the end of the century. It is well exemplified in Fried-rich von Hausen, a knight from Kreuznach in western Germany, who served under Frederick I (Barbarossa) and died on a crusade in 1190. It is through his poetry that the refined love lyric of Provence makes its entry into German literature. Heinrich von Morungen, who died in 1222, wrote poetry in which high *Minne* is sometimes celebrated with an unexpected intensity. The greatest master of this new courtly poetry is Reinmar der Alte (so called to distinguish him from a later or 'newer' Reinmar – von Zweter). Reinmar, a native probably of Hagenau in Alsace, far from being old, died in his prime about 1210. He settled at the ducal court in Vienna and made himself the acknowledged master of courtly love poetry. The success of his refined and restrained art proves that a sensitive and civilised public was there to listen to him. Since Reinmar's poetry is deliberately confined within narrow limits and its subject-matter is remote, he is not an easy poet for the modern reader, who has to adjust himself to conventions and views current only for a short period cen-turies ago. Moreover the *Minnelied* was sung and the texts which we possess were certainly not more than half the entertainment; relatively few of the tunes are known and the style can only be resurrected with difficulty; all this makes apparent how hard it is for us to penetrate to the understanding of this refined and subtle art.

The difficulties are less obvious in the poetry of Walther von der Vogelweide, partly because his self-absorption expressed itself in words and partly because by his gifts he is the greatest German lyric poet before Goethe. We know little about the facts of Walther's life, his native district is not certainly established, his social rank is in doubt, and his burial at Würzburg, though plausible, is not proved. The dates of his birth (*c.* 1170) and death (*c.* 1230) are only probable estimates. But Walther's abundant poetry makes a biography otiose. It gives no outline of his career, but in its vivid personal stamp it brings the poet to life, spotlighting his easily touched off feelings. Walther, who may have been of petty nobility, became a professional poet, singing for great lords and dependent on their patronage, and the bitterness of this life is poignantly expressed in what are usually believed to be his last poems. He began in Vienna, learning his trade from Reinmar, with whom he later fell out. He was often in the train of kings (Philip of Swabia, Otto IV and Frederick II) as well as nobles such as Landgrave Hermann of Thuringia. A vehemently committed man, Walther wrote poems commenting on political persons and events from his own decided standpoint, and these hundred or so gnomic poems, or *Sprüche*, as they are called, are among the most interesting and original of his productions. He wrote love poetry which is pure *Minnesang* in the courtly manner of Reinmar and he also wrote poems, often called *Mädchenlieder*, which have nothing to do with *Minne*, reflecting a love which is warm, earthy and realisable. He had also a style which is between the two, combining dignity and refinement with the live human relationship of the *Mädchenlieder*. What makes Walther so remarkable a figure and gives him even today so powerful an impact, is his own vivid interest and commitment, the personal directness of the poems and the extraordinary fluency and felicity of expression.

A younger contemporary of Walther, Neithart von Reuental, who probably lived from about 1185 to about 1240, abandoned the courtly *Minnesang* altogether, singing of village festivals and dancing with satirical portrayal of rural manners. Neithart brings himself into his rustic poems, underlining the peasants' hostility to the knight. This *Dörperpoesie*, as it is often called, may be regarded as a decline in poetry from the elevated plane of the courtly love song; but it can also be seen as a kind of poetry which is closer to life, robust, vigorous and imbued with caustic irony.

If the lyric could provide varied self-contained entertainment for a single occasion, the court romance had the advantage of continuity through a long succession of winter evenings, and the knightly epics, in their leisurely progress, enjoyed a repute at least as great as that of the lyric poetry. To appreciate them now it is necessary to project oneself into the age in which they were written, in order to understand the naïve sense of action, the ready response to wonder, the alert feeling for symbolism expressed in allegory, and the sophisticated awareness of manners and social relationships.

The courtly romance, like other forms of the day, derives from France, and so it is not surprising that its first appearance in German is the work of a poet from the borderland between the French and the Germanic languages: the knight Heinrich von Veldeke, a native of the region of Maastricht, lived from about 1140 to about 1210 and wrote between 1170 and 1189 an epic poem which is an adaptation of the French *Roman d'Énéas*. Veldeke's *Eneit* recounts the story of Aeneas and especially his love for Dido and Lavinia in fluent verse, notable for its pure rhymes.

In the thirty years that followed, a considerable number of romances were written and three writers of first rank emerged, Hartmann von Aue, Wolfram von Eschenbach, and Gottfried von Strassburg. Hartmann, a Swabian knight, probably from a locality which is now within the Swiss border (Eglisau), was born about 1165 and died soon after 1210. He wrote a small number of *Minne* poems, but he is chiefly known for two Arthurian epics and two shorter narrative works. The first of these four poems, *Erec*, derives from a French work by Chrétien de Troyes; it tells the Arthurian story, familiar to English readers as 'Enid and Geraint', show-ing the wedded Erec first in unknightly complacency, from which he reacts to uncourtly churlishness, until he is won over to a balanced life by the steadfast love and devotion of Enite. Hartmann's poem accords with the courtly convention that the loved woman educates and elevates the man. *Iwein*, which is Hartman's last work, completed about 1203, is formally the most perfect, and though modern readers may find it some-what cool and detached, it enjoyed considerable repute and popularity in the Middle Ages. Derived, like *Erec*, from a poem by Chrétien de Troyes, *Iwein* is an Arthurian story of sudden love, estrangement and reconciliation, with an abund-ance of adventure and exotic encounter, of which the best-known episode is Iwein's rescue of a lion, which becomes his inseparable companion.

Hartmann's two shorter works, *Gregorius* and *Der arme Heinrich*, conform to conventions more readily appreciated by a modern reader than the complex web of Arthurian romance. *Gregorius*, written probably between 1187 and 1189, is thought to be the expression of an emotional crisis in Hartmann's life, but it is not possible to do more than specu-late about its cause. It is a moving poem telling of expiation by long-endured mortification. Gregorius, unwittingly guilty of incest, discovers his sin and withdraws in anguish into the wilderness, where he spends seventeen years chained on a rocky island. This severe self-imposed penance is ended by the arrival of messengers who seek him out as the new Pope.

Hartmann's most famous narrative work, *Der arme Hein-rich*, is also his shortest. Probably written about 1195, it tells of a nobleman who, in the midst of his prosperity, is struck down by leprosy. A young girl, who has learned that his cure can only be effected by the heart's blood of a virgin, loves him to the point of insisting on being sacrificed for him. Before the fatal operation can be carried out on her, Heinrich is miraculously cured and the intending victim becomes his wife. It is a poem not only of noble simplicity but of deeply felt tenderness.

Though Wolfram von Eschenbach wrote somewhat later than Hartmann, he was probably about the same age and

29

died about 1220. Wolfram, who was of knightly rank, was probably, like Walther, a professional poet. Thanks in part to Wagner, his masterpiece *Parzival*, probably written between 1200 and 1210, has become familiar at least in title to many modern readers and listeners. Its source was *Le Conte del Graal* of Chrétien de Troyes, but Wolfram, who had a more original and independent mind than many of his contemporaries, adapted his model more boldly. In this long and complex poem, Parzival, the son of a knight brought up in ignorance of chivalry, seeks to become a knight himself and progresses by devious paths and in spite of errors and backslidings to the full ideal of chivalrous conduct, symbolised by his installation as the Grail King. It is a work of deep ethical seriousness expressed in a rugged and sometimes obscure personal style. Yet the difficulties it poses did not impede its popularity, for it seems to have been a favourite poem with the public of the thirteenth and fourteenth centuries.

Soon after completing *Parzival* Wolfram turned his attention to another French romance, now lost; the resultant poem, entitled *Willehalm*, remained unfinished. Its background is war between Christians and Saracens in southern France. Willehalm (Wilhelm), a Christian lord, is taken prisoner, but escapes with the Saracen king's daughter, Arabele, whom he marries. The Saracens invade in order to avenge the outrage and recover the princess. Since Willehalm's forces are not strong enough to conquer alone, he sets out for the French court to plead for armed help, leaving his wife, now christened Gyburg, to conduct the defence of Orange, which she accomplishes with skill and resolution. Willehalm returns with powerful forces, the city is relieved, and the Saracens defeated with great slaughter. It is a poem of the crusading Christian soldier, for whom death in war against the infidel is martyrdom leading to heavenly bliss; at the same time it shows a new chivalrous regard for a brave, though misguided, adversary. Wolfram's last work, 'Titurel', survives only in fragments; half a century later (about 1272) it was completed by another poet, calling himself Albrecht, who was possibly Albrecht von Scharfenberg. In this form it is known as *Der jüngere Titurel*.

30

That the third great epic poet of the turn of the century was a commoner, who was held in high esteem, is a sign of a widening of the social horizon. Gottfried von Strassburg, a scholar and a master of French as well as of his native tongue, died about 1210 before he could complete his only work, the romance *Tristan und Isold*, which is based on a poem by Thomas de Bretagne. After an elaborate narration explaining Isold's hostility to Tristan, the crux is reached when Tristan, having wooed Isold for King Marke, quaffs the love potion, in which Isold joins him, so that the two are overcome by irresistible mutual love. The marriage of Marke and Isold takes place, but a surreptitious liaison is maintained by Tristan and the queen. Dismissed from court, they lead an idyllic love life in the grotto of *Minne*. Allowed to return, they continue their love at court until all is discovered and Tristan is banished. Soon after this point the poem breaks off. So popular a work as this became could not be left unfinished. Completions were made by Ulrich von Türheim about 1240 and by Heinrich von Freiberg about forty years later; but their contributions fall far below the level of Gottfried's original, which in its smooth and elegant verse and in its perceptive and subtle treatment of the psychology of the two lovers has a skill and depth which imitators could not attain.

These three poets are the peaks of courtly narrative literature, and clustered round them were many works of less vision and refinement, epics like Herbort von Fritzlar's *Lied von Troja* (c. 1190), Ulrich von Zazikhofen's *Lanzelet* (c. 1195) with its philandering hero, Wirnt von Grafenberg's *Wigalois* (c. 1205) with its wise saws and extravagant adventures, or the uncertainly dated, anonymous *Moriz von Craûn* with its scandalous story and enigmatic morality.

The world of the courts, which constituted the literary public of the thirteenth century, was not inextricably entangled in the esoteric gyrations of ideal *Minne*. It had a broader taste and a perception for other modes. One of the most popular poems of that age was the lay of the Nibelungs (*Nibelungenlied*), which, though its characters display courtly manners, is heroic and tragic, evincing at times a ferocity, a martial aggressiveness and a brutality which are worlds away

31

from the polite fantasy of Arthurian romance. The ingredients from which it is brewed belong to a remote and shadowy past. But the story has been refurbished and successfully transplanted to a 'modern' environment, the knightly world of the late twelfth century. Probably it was written about 1180–90. It is in two parts. The first tells of the wooing of Brunhild by Gunther with Siegfried's secret aid, of the wooing of Kriemhild by Siegfried, of the terrible quarrel between the two queens and of the consequent murder of Siegfried by Hagen. The second part is the chronicle of Kriemhild's vengeance, culminating in the long-drawn-out slaughter in which the Nibelungs and all their kin perish to the last man – and to the last woman, for the last to fall is the avenger, Kriemhild herself. Of all the narrative poetry of the German Middle Ages the *Nibelungenlied* is the work which most readily appeals to a modern taste, by its starkness, its grim heroism and its unexpected touches of tenderness. It may be that its contemporaries saw it differently, but it is one of the touchstones of great art that it has the breadth and the multiplicity still to make its effect when the viewpoint has shifted.

The great works of the age have all a moral basis, though they do not flaunt their message. There are also writers who are intentionally and exclusively moralistic. Such is the author of *Der Winsbecke* (who himself probably bore this name), a Franconian knight writing about 1215. It is a poem in which a knight purports to address his son, and the counsel he imparts embraces the three points of the chivalric ideal – the fear of God, the true service of *Minne* and soldierly virtue. And Freidank, a commoner poet of the thirteenth century, is the author of *Die Bescheidenheit* (1215–30), a collection of verse aphorisms touching on morals viewed from the religious standpoint.

4. The Later Middle Ages: 1230–1500

The structure of the courtly world, as it is seen in literature, was fragile, composed of genuine ethical values and highly artificial conventions poised in delicate balance. The poetry of the age which followed lost some of its high seriousness and inclined more and more frankly to entertainment. The old poems continued to command an attentive public, but the new generation turned to multiplicity of adventure and richness of adornment.

At first the heroic epic seems to have been little affected, perhaps because it was the form which came closest to life. *Kudrun*, written about 1230, the story of a persecuted princess who in the end escapes from bondage, has episodes of imaginative vision which momentarily put it on the level of the *Nibelungenlied*. But the heroic epics of the following generation, *Ortnit* and its sequel *Wolfdietrich*, written about 1250, turn more and more to story-telling, to the neglect of character creation.

The year 1250, in which the Emperor Frederick II died, ended a political era in Germany. Though Frederick was virtually an Italian and was only twice in Germany, he was the last Emperor of the house of Staufen which had ruled for more than a century (since 1138) and had seen the rise and witnessed the first signs of the weakening of the chivalric ideal. The knight was now on the decline. His warlike prowess was undiminished, but the aura of religious dedication was fading. Jerusalem fell in 1244 and Acre in 1291, and these disasters point to the end of two centuries of religious militarism. And as the knight secularised himself, other orders of society, and notably the burghers of the prosperous towns, began to stir into self-consciousness.

Meanwhile the courts continued to enjoy the entertainment of *Minnesang* and verse romance. Gottfried von Neifen, who lived in the first half of the thirteenth century, adorned his poetry with sensual images while still respecting the conventional abstinence of the *Minne* tradition. Ulrich von Lichtenstein, a mettlesome knight of Styria, who died about 1275, connected his poems in his *Frauendienst* by a narrative (possibly autobiographical), virtually turning *Minne* into a sport like his favourite pastime of jousting. On the other hand Reinmar von Zweter, who was chiefly active in Bohemia (1230–60?), turned his back on *Minne* and concentrated his *Spruch* poems on honour (Frau Ehre).

B   33

The two principal practitioners of extended poetry in the years following the great days of Wolfram and Gottfried were Rudolf von Ems and Konrad von Würzburg. Rudolf, a younger contemporary of the great writers of the turn of the century, wrote his poems between 1220 and 1250 and died in Italy in 1252 or 1253. Of his six substantial narrative poems five have survived. *Der gute Gerhard*, unexpectedly foreshadowing a distant future, has as its hero a merchant commoner, a man of integrity and humility. The principal character of *Barlaam und Josaphat*, a romance with oriental origins, achieves peace by renouncing the flesh and devoting himself to communion with God. In *Willehalm von Orlens* Rudolf reverts to the Arthurian romance of the late twelfth century. His last two works, both of which remained unfinished, were planned on an immense scale. His *Alexander* portrays the Macedonian king as an ideal ruler, and his *Weltchronik*, a formidable fragment of 36,000 lines, is a medieval project of history which works its way through biblical and classical times and breaks off even before it reaches the Christian era. Though Rudolf had neither the depth nor the originality of his predecessors, he lacked neither skill nor learning, and in the thirteenth century, with its high esteem for craftsmanship, he ranked as one of the first of the poets.

Konrad von Würzburg, who belonged to the next generation, being born about 1225 and dying in 1287, is a brilliant example of the craftsman poet. The age cared little for originality. Just as it did not expect from the goldsmith or the armourer originality, but skilful workmanship and ingenious detail, so it looked to the poet for expertness in the fashioning of intricate patterns of verse. Konrad, a professional poet living a large part of his life in Basel, possessed a remarkably versatile talent, writing *Minnesang, Spruch* poems, allegories, short verse romances, heraldic poetry and verse legends, as well as three long narrative poems. Of the shorter romances the most notable are *Das Herzemaere* and *Der Schwanritter*. The former tells a tale of illicit love, and though the incident in which the lover's heart is served up as a meal to his unwitting mistress is repugnant to a modern taste, it portrays the erring woman's sad end with decorous sympathy. *Der*

Schwanritter, an unfinished romance, tells the story of Lohen-grin; and *Das Turnier von Nantes* describes an imaginary tournament with a wealth of heraldic detail. The analogy of Konrad's work to the detailed art of the goldsmith is rein-forced by his decorative hymn to the Virgin Mary, which is significantly entitled *Die goldene Schmiede*. Konrad's three longer romances, *Engelhard, Partonopier und Meliur* and *Der Trojanerkrieg* (which, though unfinished, reaches 40,000 lines) are laid out on a scale at which his manner is no longer effective. His merit is his ornate style (*geblümte Rede*, as he called it), which unfolds itself in elegant detail; he had not the gift of shaping a large-scale work. But for a public ready to listen to a long story in numerous short instalments, this display of detailed perfection could be as acceptable as the grand sweep of a work unified by an original mind.

The outlook of society in the thirteenth century was firmly Christian; but the focus shifted steadily to the things of the world. The courtly society saw literature as a fine art, a form of pleasurable craftsmanship. But it also turned to books for the rules of social behaviour and began to develop an interest for realistic and scurrilous story-telling. *Der wälsche Gast*, written in 1215–16 by Thomasin von Circlaere (Cerchiari in Italy), sets out the principles of a virtuous life, including such practical matters as advice on deportment and table manners. The civilisation of Italy takes a hold in Germany, for this book by an Italian priest writing in a foreign tongue ('ein welscher Gast') was widely distributed and continued to be read by later generations of the Middle Ages. Equally popular was *Der Renner* (*c.* 1300), an immense moral poem by Hugo von Trimberg dealing exhaustively with the seven deadly sins. Its length (25,000 lines) was no bar for an age with no sense of haste.

About the middle of the thirteenth century a literature of realistic detail began to appear, heralded by two poems, which may have been written by the same author. *Die böse Frau* is a lament by a harried husband, *Der Weinschwelg* a humor-ous poem in praise of wine. About half a century later another short poem, *Das Kotzemaere*, tells in realistic terms an epi-sode of filial ingratitude cured by childlike simplicity. And

35

the same tradition of moral writing by anecdote is followed in an engaging cat fable (*Von der katzen*) written by Herrand von Wildonie in the late thirteenth century.

The growth of a simpler and more homely literature did not mean that *Minnesang* with its stylised elegance was dead. Indeed, in the eyes of contemporaries it rose to new heights in the late thirteenth century in the work of Heinrich Frauenlob, who was probably born about 1250–60 and died in 1318. Frauenlob was a highly successful professional poet, who was courted and lauded by the great and influential. His prolific poetry, principally composed of *Spruch* poems, though it includes some *Minnelieder*, is written in an elaborate mannerist style, which exactly caught the taste of the age. It was just after Frauenlob's time that the most beautiful manuscript of German medieval poetry was executed, the lavish *Grosse Heidelberger* or *Manessische Handschrift* with its exquisite (imaginary) portraits of the poets. Done to the commission of rich collectors in Zürich, it was a sign that the *Minnesang* was losing its original vitality and becoming a kind of *objet d'art* for the well-to-do connoisseur. Hadamar von Laber's poetic allegory of love under the image of the hunt (*Die Jagd, c.* 1340) is perhaps a last echo of the rich and refined courtly life of the Staufen epoch.

The new age which began to shape itself in the thirteenth century and was fully apparent in the fourteenth was beset with tensions. Social attitudes shifted, values changed. People were perhaps not coarser or more materialistic than they had been half a century before. But the idealistic standards which had once been accepted were questioned and breached. A new generation put its trust in money, property and sensual gratification – and saw no wrong in doing so. Already the poem *Meier Helmbrecht* (*c.* 1250–80) by Wernher der Gartemaere had revealed the shift in social values; for the farmer's son attempts to act the knight, declines into brutal criminality and finds a miserable end. And an unknown author, erroneously called Seifried Helblinc, castigates in his fifteen poems the ways of a world which has lost its integrity, giving itself up to ostentation and deceit. The age of the amoral tale begins, in which the cunning triumph and the fools are fleeced. Among

36

the first of these anecdotal narratives is the cycle of *Der Pfaffe Amis* (*c.* 1250), attributed to Der Stricker. Over and over again Amis mocks at and scores off a slow-witted 'Establishment'.

In face of this increasing amoralisation, clerics, including gifted and popular preachers, foremost among them Berthold von Regensburg (*c.* 1215–72), denounced the growing corruption and admonished their hearers to an honest and humble Christian life. And a generation or more later the great mystics Meister Eckhart (*c.* 1260–1327), Heinrich Seuse (*c.* 1293–1366) and Johannes Tauler (*c.* 1300–61) turned away from the sensual and material world to the inner life of the soul in unity with God.

Conditions in the middle of the fourteenth century led to a sharpening of the contrasts and conflicts of the time. From 1347 to 1350 the Black Death swept through Europe, extinguishing villages and depleting towns. And the renewed awareness of death in the midst of life, engendered by this terrible visitation and by further plague years at frequent intervals, drove men either into a religious flight from the world or to a desperate enjoyment and exploitation of a precarious existence. One of the finest formulations of this situation of the individual in face of death and affliction is *Der Ackermann aus Böhmen*, a rhythmical prose dialogue written about 1400 by Johann von Saaz in the form of a complaint at law. The ploughman, who has lost his wife, arraigns death before God's throne, loses his suit, and is admonished to resignation and humility.

In the fifteenth century, in which the malaise and misgovernment of Germany became more and more acute, the voice of the realistic, crass and drastic satirist was heard with increasing insistence. Heinrich Wittenweiler's *Ring*, a savage and partly obscene satirical poem written early in the century, trounces the peasant and does not spare the knight. And the Low German poem of *Reinke de Vos* ('Reynard the Fox'), published in 1498, is an amusing and cynical exposure of a world in which there are clever knaves and stupid knaves but no honest men, a world in which power and possessions alone count. And when a lyric poet appears in Oswald von Wolkenstein (1377–1445), he is no longer a knightly *Minnesänger* stylising his life, but a turbulent, violent character using the conventional forms for a vivid expression of his own tempestuous career.

The Middle Ages closed in moral confusion, political chaos and religious uncertainty. The laity was without direction, the princes had jettisoned responsibility for self-interest, and the vices of the world and the pursuit of power had bitten deep into the Church, which seemed powerless to reform itself. *Das Narrenschiff*, published in 1494 by Sebastian Brant (1457–1521), a minor official in Strasburg, exposes the public and private follies of the time, providing a final summary of the Middle Ages and giving a hint of a new age to come.

3 The Sixteenth Century

Towards the end of the fifteenth century the chivalric world seemed for a moment to give a flickering promise of renewal. The Habsburg Emperor Maximilian I (1459–1519), who came to the throne in 1486, saw himself in his private fantasy as a knight battling against evil and he commissioned two large, handsome, illustrated works which should portray him in the image of a knightly hero. *Teuerdank* (1517), written in verse by Melchior Pfinzing (1481–1535), depicts Maximilian's journey to the Netherlands to seek his bride Marie of Burgundy, disguising it beneath a wealth of imaginary episodes, in which Teuerdank-Maximilian is repeatedly beset by three miscreants whom he in the end triumphantly destroys. *Der Weisskunig*, which was in part the work of Maximilian himself, remained unfinished and was not printed until 1775. The unreality of these two fantastic anachronisms only served to show that the world of the knight had outlived itself. They are steeped in an archaising romanticism which looks back nostalgically to an age which is irrevocably lost. It is perhaps symbolical that 'the last knight', as Maximilian was called, was almost uniformly unsuccessful in the practical world of politics.

A generation earlier a new invention had opened possibilities which were only gradually perceived but were of the farthest-reaching consequence. Printing by slow and cumbersome methods was already known; but Gutenberg's movable metal type letters offered the prospect of an immense extension of the printing process, and within forty years of his death in 1468 the maximum size of printings had risen from 150 to more than 1000. This acceleration of the technique and its consequent cheapening opened the way for an enormous extension of publication with ever-widening social repercussions.

The humanism of Italy had begun to be imported into

Germany in the fifteenth century, partly through the coming together of Churchmen at the great international ecclesiastical councils of Constance (1414–18) and Basel (1431–49). As the century progressed its spread and growth were greatly expedited by the new invention of printing. The new unobstructed vision of Latin and, to a lesser extent, of Greek literature evoked a fresh conception of the ancient world, revealing forgotten power and harmony. The first studies of the New Learning were fostered by men of education who were at first mainly functionaries and administrators in flourishing commercial cities. Among them were Niklas von Wyle (1410–c. 1479) of Nürnberg, Heinrich Steinhöwel (1412–82) of Ulm and Albrecht von Eyb (1420–75), a canon of Bamberg, who all wrote fluently in Latin and endeavoured to impart to their German writings a classical dexterity and ease.

The late fifteenth and early sixteenth centuries were a time of the multiplication and expansion of universities, which served as nurseries to the new humanism; and the humanists of the next generation were very different from the respectable and thoughtful men of affairs who had gone before them. The new men were for the most part restless figures flitting from university to university, with a pride in their distinction as scholars which not infrequently swelled into intolerant arrogance. The most famous of them, Konrad Celtis (1459–1508), whose real name was Bickel, was as mobile as any, appearing at different times in Rostock, Erfurt, Leipzig, Nürnberg, Rome, Venice, Cracow, Regensburg and Ingolstadt. As he passed from place to place he founded literary societies, some of which prospered and exercised considerable influence. Celtis ignored German and wrote only in Latin, skilfully composing verse which includes much love poetry which some have thought to be autobiographical. His alert and restless energy was rewarded with some remarkable discoveries of lost works, including the Latin plays of the medieval nun Hrotswith (see above, p. 15) and a Roman atlas of Europe (*Tabula Peutingeriana*), What the literary achievements of humanism might have been in Germany no one can tell, for the eruption of powerful new forces soon diverted into religious channels the energies of the most gifted humanists.

Of these the most notable by far is Desiderius Erasmus (1469–1536), not a German but an international figure, born in Rotterdam and equally at home in London, where he visited Sir Thomas More, and in Basel, where he spent much of his later life. He also paid long visits to Italy and to Paris, and when the Reformation broke out in Basel, he took refuge for a time in Freiburg. Erasmus, who wrote in Latin, was a man of thorough learning, reflected in his scholarly writings, and possessed also an urbane, highly civilised and eminently clear mind. He saw the need and the urgency for ecclesiastical reform and he sympathised with and supported the early steps taken by Luther. In the end he was repelled by the coarseness and short-sightedness of the reform movement and was especially concerned at the division of the Christian world for which the Reformation seemed to be heading. As the theological hurly-burly grew, the voice of moderates, such as Erasmus, drew less and less attention.

Johann Reuchlin (1455–1522), the first great German humanist of the sixteenth century, also found himself, through his very tolerance and impartiality, embroiled in religious controversy with a narrow Catholic faction in Cologne. The battle was won for Reuchlin by his supporters, who published the *Epistolae obscurorum virorum* (or *Dunkelmännerbriefe*, 1515–17), a savage satire in the form of fictitious Latin letters. Reuchlin died before the course of the reform movement was clear, but his intelligence, humanity and moral integrity would probably have led him to an attitude similar to that of Erasmus. Ulrich von Hutten (1488–1523), who in his early life was a wandering scholar and a mercenary soldier, was one of Reuchlin's adherents in the Cologne controversy and was all his short life entangled by his stormy temperament in fierce conflicts and hazardous enterprises, ending as a mortally sick refugee in Switzerland. Hutten stands out from the more pacific humanists by his pugnacity and also by his willingness to use German instead of Latin in his later satirical writings.

These three humanists of such differing temperament were all linked with the background to reform rather than with the Reformation itself. The movement for the reform of the Church was not new; it extended back at least to the beginning of the fifteenth century. Though nominally one body, the Church was seriously divided within, for on the one hand the consciousness of its mission of piety was widespread, while on the other hand the opportunities for exercise of power and the acquisition of wealth drew to it many, especially among the nobility, who had no kind of vocation. The Papacy, from the moment of its assertion of political power in the eleventh century, had paid for its power by an ever-increasing worldliness, and had profited from the worldliness by ever-increasing wealth. Noble families acquired the actual or virtual patronage over ecclesiastical offices and used them to provide for younger sons. Many of the monasteries forgot their high mission, and a proportion of the parish clergy imitated the vices of their seniors.

Corruption and neglect, however, were only one half of the picture. Without intense and widespread religious feeling the Reformation could never have developed into a formidable revolutionary movement. It was the active consciousness of the true religious life which caused the vices and abuses to be so deeply resented. Certainly political forces were also implicated in the new trend and the territorial princes soon saw in the new movement a chance to augment power and accumulate wealth; but the main driving force was an intense religious conviction.

The Reformation, when it came, developed out of a comparatively minor incident. Martin Luther (1483–1546), a monk seconded as a professor to the young University of Wittenberg, grew indignant at a high-powered and particularly shameless fund-raising campaign – the sale of indulgences. On 31 October 1517 he nailed to the door of the Castle Church at Wittenberg his 95 *Thesen* of protest. Out of this personal demonstration grew, through the intransigence of the opposition and Luther's own dynamism, the tremendous movement which divided the Church and with it Germany. By 1521 the survival of Protestantism was assured; Luther had faced the Diet of Worms and found princely support, and his supporters and followers were to be found in numbers in every part of Germany.

It is remarkable that Luther, besides being one of the key

42

figures in European history, should also have been a moulding force in German literature, for his interest in accepted literary forms was slender. His prose writings are almost all utilitarian, exhortations or admonitions or affirmations, such as the three important tracts written in 1520, *An den christlichen Adel deutscher Nation, De captivitate Babylonica* and *Von der Freiheit eines Christenmenschen.* Even his robust hymns are functional in the sense that they are intended to provide the new Church with a suitable stock of hymnary material. Luther's greatest achievement is his translation of the Bible, accomplished between 1521 and 1534 with the aim of furnishing the common man with a Bible written in language that he could understand. The result is a book which has not only had an immense spiritual influence but has also by its cadences, its vocabulary and its images had an immeasurable effect on creative writing in Germany at least as far as the nineteenth century. The common-sense principles on which Luther based his homely and vivid translation are bluntly enunciated in the tract *Ein Sendbrief vom Dolmetschen* (1530), in which he insists on observation of the language spoken in houses, streets and markets.

But the enormous creative impulse which Luther bestowed through this single channel on the German language had to be paid for. The intense focus upon the Bible implied a loss in other intellectual fields. And the unstable balance between the new Church and the old absorbed for a critical generation the energies and intelligence of the best minds. For the Reformation was neither won nor lost. The initial impetus of its expansion flagged, Catholicism by the Counter-Reformation eventually regained some of the lost ground, and an uneasy cold war persisted, in which the interchange of religious propaganda, conducted in terms of the utmost crudity and virulence, never ceased. Moreover the new religion became as intolerant and as exclusive as the old, persecuting sects of great sincerity and piety, such as the Anabaptists, and sharply denouncing (in Luther's *Wider die räuberischen and mörderischen Rotten der Bauern,* 1525) the political consequences which, in the Peasants' War, the common man drew from the new doctrines.

In this world in which the men of learning either withdrew

into the ivory tower of neo-Latin poetry or freely spent their energies in the hurly-burly of sulphurous theological polemics, it was the burghers of the prosperous commercial towns, such as Nürnberg and Augsburg, who found the leisure and inclination for poetic writing. The outstanding figure (no doubt in part thanks to Wagner's *Die Meistersinger von Nürnberg*) is for us the Nürnberg cobbler Hans Sachs (1494–1576). Sachs was an adept at *Meistersang*, but Wagner's tendentious advocacy should not delude us into overestimating its prestige or its poetry. Taken very seriously only by a small, esoteric circle of burghers, it was little more than a petrified relic of *Minnesang*. Hans Sachs' main gift was for the crisp, humorous or salty anecdote, which he presented in short, robust plays called *Fastnachtspiele*, written in rather knobbly, short-lined irregular verse going by the name of *Knittelverse*. In all he wrote some 200 of these. For all his inexhaustible resourcefulness he is no key figure in the development of German drama or poetry, because these plays, written for a public with narrow horizons, were themselves parochial and lacked any broader vision. The figure of Sachs only became widely influential when, in the latter part of the eighteenth century, Goethe created of him a personal image of bonhomie, bluntness, good humour and mature wisdom, which may have corresponded to Sachs the man, but had little to do with what he wrote.

Writers such as Sachs existed in other German cities, and one such was Jörg Wickram (*c.* 1500–*c.* 1560) of Colmar in Alsace. Wickram tried his hand at novels as well as plays and left, as his characteristic work, a collection of anecdotes, amusing, scurrilous or instructive, intended for the entertainment of travellers and therefore entitled *Das Rollwagenbüchlein* (1555).

Not far removed from this quaint and rather pedestrian citizen literature are the anonymous poems and stories which we call *Volkslieder* and *Volksbücher*. The simple and unpretentious scope of the *Volkslied* was capable of a purer and higher vision than the citizen poets mostly achieved. They were aiming at instruction or entertainment, whereas in the folk-songs music was as important as words and the singers wanted only to feel, not to teach. It was in this century that some of the most attractive German *Volkslieder* were recorded, including the carol 'Es ist ein' Ros' entsprungen', the well-known farewell to Innsbruck, 'Innsbruck, ich muss dich lassen', the drinking song 'Der liebste Buhle, den ich han' and 'Zwischen Berg und tiefem Tal'. The chapbooks or *Volksbücher* were homely, artless narrations written to supply the need of a new class of unpretentious readers in the towns. They retold, in prose, tales which the Middle Ages had known as verse romances (e.g. *Der hürnen Seyfried*, Siegfried's story); they picked up subjects from the new short narrative literature of Italy (e.g. *Griseldis*); or they drew on topical or recent events, combining them with traditional themes, as in the *Faustbuch* of 1587 (the life of the real Faust and the story of the man who sells his soul to the devil). This *Faustbuch*, which in many respects is a dreary moral tract, had a story so potent that it fructified in English literature (Marlowe), and much more widely in German. In the same tradition of burgher literature as the *Volksbücher* were the collections of comic anecdotes concentrated either on a place (*Das Lalebuch*, 1597, relocated at Schilda in *Die Schildbürger*, 1598) or on a single popular trickster hero such as *Till Eulenspiegel*, which first appeared in 1478, but retained its popularity through the sixteenth century and was reissued in verse by Fischart (see below) in 1572. Even the humanist tradition adapted itself to the burghers' outlook when Georg Rollenhagen (1542–1609) turned the classical tale of the war between the frogs and the mice into a popular beast epic (*Der Froschmeuseler*, 1595). A similar fusion of the classical and the popular was achieved when the social satire *Grobianus* (1549) by Friedrich Dedekind (c. 1525–98), a Latin castigation of the coarse manners of the age, was successfully turned into German in 1551 by Kaspar Scheidt (c. 1520–65). Through this poem Grobianus became a proverbial symbolical figure for many decades.

It was perhaps not surprising that this contentious and combative century was an age of successful satire. One of its masters was Lutheran Johann Fischart (1546–90), who began with anti-Catholic satires, including *Der Barfüssersecten und Kuttenstreit* (1570), but then extended his range to more general satire. He denounced prophesying almanacs in *Aller Praktik Grossmutter* (1572), and castigated women in *Der Flöhhatz* (1573). His masterpiece is his free adaptation of Rabelais' *Gargantua et Pantagruel*, first issued in 1575 and known since its second edition in 1582 as *Geschichtklitterung*. Rabelais is here enormously expanded and turned into a critical and satirical review of Fischart's times.

The drama of the sixteenth century hardly anywhere rose above a narrow provincial level. The homely short plays of Hans Sachs are mostly anecdotes in dialogue; where they attempt a higher flight, their limitations of imagination and expression reduce them to quaint relics of a pedestrian citizen culture. A fellow-townsman of Sachs, Jakob Ayrer (*c.* 1540–1605), wrote over a hundred plays in a single decade, 1592–1602. And this immense quantity is in itself a judgement on their merit. They include comedies and tragedies and range over historical subjects, medieval romances and Shakespearean plots drawn from Italian Renaissance sources. One of them (*Julius Redivivus*) is a German adaptation of a Latin play by Nikodemus Frischlin (1547–90), the last stormy petrel among the German humanists. So humanism, as it faded, had its impact on the German drama, too. An intelligent and strong-willed prince, Duke Heinrich Julius of Brunswick (1564–1613) witnessed in 1592 performances at Brunswick by a troupe of English actors playing Elizabethan dramas. So strong was the impression they made that Heinrich Julius immediately devoted himself to play-writing, producing ten plays in 1593 and 1594. They are moral dramas, exposing and punishing vice, crime and deceit, and doing so with plenty of crass and bloody scenes and broad effects of realistic comedy. And so the century ends with a debased echo of Elizabethan blood and thunder.

German literature of the sixteenth century can be a fascinating field for the specialist, but the reader with general interests will encounter disappointment. Hans Sachs and the Nürnbergers offer the charm of quaintness, which was certainly not part of their original intention. The chapbooks have a racy vigour to which the present-day reader, as well as his sixteenth-century predecessor, can respond. But in general the impres-

46

sion of something home-made, improvised, is inescapable. There seem to be several reasons for these limitations. Since Germany had neither political nor cultural centre, the new humanism was restricted to the universities, where Latin was the sole medium of teaching and of disputation; so a new and vigorous impulse was channelled into a 'dead' foreign tongue, failing to fertilise the growth of a German Renaissance literature. The towns, small in size and self-enclosed, bred only a restricted and short-range literature for a small public which could not possibly be outward-looking. And finally the Reformation, beginning in Germany, spreading in Germany, and yet not conquering Germany entirely, drew to itself the attention of most of the best minds, so that religious and especially controversial religious tracts occupy what must seem to be a disproportionately large place in the writings of many men of that age, beginning with Luther himself. To the men of that day our perspective would seem a false one. For them these questions so desperately argued were matters of the utmost moment, affecting the salvation or damnation of human souls. The personalities so savagely vilified were conceived as agents of the Devil, bent on man's destruction. Now that the heat has evaporated from the debates, the surviving works of controversy must stand by the quality and integrity of their satirical style, and this is manifestly too often distorted and strained. From this tremendous clash of spiritual and intellectual energies one positive work stands out as the supreme unshakeable achievement of the German sixteenth century, the Lutheran Bible.

4 The Seventeenth Century

There is no sharp demarcation between the sixteenth century and the seventeenth. Indeed the first fifteen years or so of the new century seem to be no more than an ebbing continuation of the last, a literary lull. What gives the new age its special tone is on the one hand the background of large-scale war accompanied by pestilence, and on the other the concentration of intellectual life in the hands of the aristocracy and its numerous counsellors and administrators.

Three events serve as symbolical heralds to the new scene. In 1617 a linguistic and literary society called *Die Fruchtbringende Gesellschaft*[1] was formed, and its founder and original members were almost exclusively noblemen. In 1618 indignant Bohemian Protestants in Prague threw the Imperial representatives out of the castle windows into the moat below, so beginning the long and destructive struggle of the Thirty Years War. Thirdly, in 1624 Martin Opitz published his *Buch von der deutschen Poeterey*, which established his dogmatic authority for half a century. The establishment of *Die Fruchtbringende Gesellschaft* and the acceptance of Opitz's little poetic treatise emphasise the authoritarian, aristocratic tone of intellectual life; and between these two pacific and literary dates, in a characteristic seventeenth-century antithesis, is sandwiched a historic event which was gradually to bring protracted suffering to hundreds of thousands.

Initially the Thirty Years War was a war of religions, the climax of the Counter-Reformation, the last attempt of the Catholic Habsburgs to impose their own religious solution upon the Empire. As it dragged on and on its issues became obscured, ambitious men exploited it for their own ends, and

[1] See below, p. 54.

foreign powers took a hand in order to augment their power and extend their possessions. Germany, and especially the common people of Germany, was caught up in an apparently unending sequence of harassment, rapine and destruction. The poetic reflection of the war can be found in Grimmelshausen's *Der abenteuerliche Simplicissimus*,[1] its graphic reproduction in *Les misères de la guerre* by the Frenchman Jacques Callot. Of course the horrors were not continuous in one place. The armies came, plundered, slaughtered and passed on. But the cumulative impoverishment wore down the rural population, reducing it to near-starvation, while the towns, occasionally caught up in ferocious atrocities like the sack of Magdeburg in 1631, lost many of their inhabitants and more of their prosperity. Communications, become unsafe, withered away, and the intellectual impulse of the universities, mainstays of poetic as well as scholarly activity, faltered. The courts alone retained something of their brilliance and offered a refuge for art and literature, and many of the writers of the age were officials at princely courts. Elsewhere poetry was overshadowed by insistent proofs of the insecurity and brevity of life. The note of *memento mori* makes its appearance in the new guise of *vanitas vanitatum*, offset only by the unpredictable and impermanent gifts of Fortuna. Moreover, the recurring horrors of reality rendered large sections of the public unresponsive to all but the most violent of stimuli.

The seemingly interminable war came to an end in the Peace of Westphalia in 1648, a settlement which emphasised the monarchical character of government and the divine sanction of the monarch. It left a weak Empire and a multiplicity of sovereign states; and this fragmentation obstructed, not only political development but also the growth of sizeable cities which could offer a soil for the fruitful unfolding of a living literature. This is certainly one reason why in the second half of the century German writing has often a heavy-handedness and a provincial narrowness which contrast unfavourably with France or England.

The century had begun in a climate which leaned towards mysticism and, on a lower level, towards superstition. A sin-

[1] See below, p. 57.

cere and glowing piety was seen in many people, often in the humblest ranks of society. It found its highest expression in the writings of Jacob Böhme (1575–1624), a self-educated Silesian cobbler who, notwithstanding obstacles and persecution, wrote towards the end of his life a series of mystical tracts, beginning in 1612 with *Aurora oder Morgenröte im Aufgang* (not published until 1634) and continuing through *Die drei Prinzipien göttlichen Wesens* (1619) to his *Mysterium magnum* of 1623. Böhme's devout yet pantheistically based piety is expressed in an obscure, heavily metaphorical language, the roots of which go back to Luther's biblical prose. Böhme may be likened to a more introspective and brooding Bunyan, and like Bunyan he touched a common chord to which many responded in the tribulations of the age.

A sense of mystery working at a much lower level animated the belief in witchcraft, so widespread in the seventeenth century. Though witches had from time to time been burned in earlier times, it was just as the Middle Ages faded that a wave of prosecutions, inquisitions and witch-burnings began to spread over Europe, symbolised by the publication in 1489 of the notorious *Malleus maleficarum* (or 'Witches' hammer') of the Dominican monks Heinrich Institoris and Jakob Sprenger. Feverish persecution intensified in the late sixteenth century and became in the seventeenth a form of mass hysteria. Among the few who dared to raise their voices against this epidemic of insensate cruelty was the Jesuit father and poet Friedrich von Spee (1591–1635), one of whose duties it was to prepare the condemned women for their end. His courageous protest against witch hunts is contained in *Cautio criminalis* (1631), written in Latin and translated into German in 1649. A man of piety and charity, Spee died of plague contracted while tending the sick. His fresh and attractive poetry, contained in *Trutznachtigall*, published in 1649 after his death, is entirely religious, uniting a simple gravity with a feeling for birds, animals and flowers unusual in that age.

Georg Rudolf Weckherlin (1584–1653), though older than Friedrich von Spee, wrote poetry which foreshadows more clearly the coming age. A man of education, and familiar with high society, he settled in London, serving first the royal then

50

the Commonwealth government and, in the last year of his life, assisting Milton, the 'Latin Secretary', in his incipient blindness. Some of Weckherlin's verse is ceremonial poetry, odes celebrating festivals or funerals; all of it has a certain pomp and elevation, an assured use of rhetorical technique and an aristocratic flair.

Thirteen years younger than Weckherlin, who was living remote in self-chosen exile, Martin Opitz (1597–1639), a Silesian without conspicuous poetic gifts, succeeded by his talent for organisation and propaganda and by his readiness to accept a limited and easily understood goal in impressing his stamp upon the next generation in German literature and directing its course. Opitz, whose volume *Teutsche Poemata* (1624) includes poems by others as well as himself, wrote deft, fluent, intelligent poetry with little imaginative power. His hastily written[1] *Buch von der deutschen Poeterey* (1624), a rapid survey of the genres of literature and of the applicability of its verse forms, was accepted by many of his contemporaries as a binding authority. This short essay in literary aesthetics is especially important, firstly for Opitz' championship of the alexandrine (twelve- or thirteen-syllabled rhyming couplets already well established in French literature), and secondly for his assertion of the suitability of the German language for poetic expression, at a moment when the educated were looking to French or (in universities) to Latin. If Opitz lacked depth, he was energetic, clear-sighted and unambiguous; and by industrious translation he enriched the scope of German literature with foreign models, including John Barclay's Latin political novel *Argenis* and Sir Philip Sidney's *Arcadia*.

Opitz stands on the threshold of a phase in German literature which is often called Baroque, though this term was unknown to his age. 'Baroque' was formerly employed for painting, sculpture and architecture and its modern use was made fashionable by the art historian Heinrich Wölfflin in *Kunstgeschichtliche Grundbegriffe* (1915). Though it is now firmly established also as a literary term, its application fluctuates, focusing at one moment on the central part of the

---

[1] Opitz claimed that he wrote it in five days ('Denn ich vor fünff tagen, wie meine Freunde wissen, die feder erst angesetzt habe').

seventeenth century, extending at another to cover the whole of the seventeenth and a part of the eighteenth, and restricted, in a third interpretation, to roughly the years 1590–1640. So mobile a term can only be of limited value, and it is better to abandon the attempt to speak of a 'Baroque period' and to employ the word as a useful blanket term to denote features of style and outlook. A fundamental characteristic of this style is sharp, even harsh, contrast. It was an age of oppositions, when many grasped at sensual pleasure before the threatening horror of disease and death. Baroque literature, moreover, is public and therefore leans to ostentation. Even the lyric poet is conscious of an audience and 'stages' a performance. And this is achieved by a lavish use of rhetorical procedures, especially antithesis and accumulation, and by an inflationary use of language which in extreme instances turns into bombast.

Beside this literature of parade and display there lived on a tradition of popular writing, descended from the sixteenth century. Some poets wrote directly, simply and unpretentiously, and the finest of the novels are those which are most popular in style. Not that the writers lived in sealed compartments; Baroque poets might show popular touches and popular authors use Baroque forms.

After Spee and Weckherlin, whose lives isolated them from other German poets, a new generation began to write in the 1630s. The new writers were numerous and gregarious. Those whose poems we still read were mostly the leaders of whole groups of sociable, companionable poets. So Simon Dach (1605–59), a professor of Königsberg, was surrounded by a 'Königsberg school' of poets, of which Dach's friend, the composer Heinrich Albert (1604–51), was the organiser and social focus. Dach, whose melancholy personality fuses with his piety in his poetry, wrote many poems to order for betrothals, weddings or funerals, and it is typical of this age of dignified or dramatic posture that these made-to-measure odes are often just as good and as sincere as Dach's more spontaneous work. He did not allow the personal links of such bespoke poetry to distract him from genuine and moving reflections on human happiness or mortality. The well-known song 'Ännchen von Tharau', which used to be attributed to Dach, but is perhaps

52

by Albert, is still sung as a 'folk-song'; and yet, in its original Low German form, 'Anke van Tharaw', it was a poem written to order, a proof that simple expressiveness can be achieved without spontaneity. Paul Fleming (1609–40), a doctor who, in an adventurous early life, travelled into Russia and Persia, wrote poems combining a deeply personal note with the stylistic formality of Opitz. And Johann Rist (1607–71), a pastor at Wedel near Hamburg and a prolific poet, who also took Opitz as a model, contrived in such a hymn as 'O Ewigkeit, du Donnerwort' to blend awe and homely piety.

Most of all the simple popular note is heard in the great mass of poems composed and set to music for use in Church services. The greatest writer of hymns in the seventeenth century was the Protestant pastor Paul Gerhardt (1607–76), a man of moral courage, who accepted dismissal from his Berlin parish rather than compromise a principle. Gerhardt's hymns have a direct warmth of feeling and an unsentimental sensitivity. The best-known of all these poems, many of which have survived to the present day, is the 'Abendlied' ('Nun ruhen alle Wälder'); while in 'O Haupt voll Blut und Wunden' Gerhardt made an exceptionally felicitous translation of a Latin hymn by St Bernard of Clairvaux.

Johann Scheffler (1624–77), a Silesian physician who used the pseudonym Angelus Silesius ('the Silesian Messenger'), belonged to the Catholic side of the confessional divide. Though brought up a Lutheran, he became a convert about the age of thirty. An active polemical writer in the religious field, he published his tracts over his real name. By using his pseudonym exclusively for his poetry he showed how completely separate were his two kinds of writing. Scheffler's principal poetic work is *Der cherubinische Wandersmann* (1675), a collection of mystical epigrams which match Gerhardt's Protestant hymns in sincerity, yet in form evince a Baroque delight in antithesis and paradox.

The stylistic density required in epigram and its leaning to oxymoron and paradox commended this form to other seventeenth-century writers, of whom the most notable was Friedrich von Logau (1604–55), also a Silesian, who spent his life in princely service in Liegnitz. Logau's *Deutscher Sinnge-*

dichte drei Tausend (1653) succeeds in its wide-ranging, cumulative epigrams in holding up a satirical mirror to the social and political face of his age.

Some of the poets had relatively little to say, but compensated by a sense of style and an interest in the values of words. Since such formalists tend to mark stages of historical development, they are sometimes more readily remembered than more weighty writers. One such was the Nürnberger Georg Philipp Harsdörffer (1607–58), who wrote pastoral poetry and hymns, displaying a real talent for the manipulation and accumulation of words. Christian Hofmann von Hofmannswaldau (1617–79), an important official in the Silesian city of Breslau, developed a mastery of many verse forms, showing his facility especially in sonnets and epistles in alexandrine verse. And Philip von Zesen (1619–89), who spent a substantial part of his life in Holland, ending up in Hamburg, had an absorbing interest in words, which he used inventively in his poetry. A man of independent ideas and strong will, Zesen devoted his life to an unsuccessful campaign for spelling reform. He is also the author of two once popular novels, *Die adriatische Rosamund* (1645) and *Assenat* (1670).

Several of these poets (Opitz, Harsdörffer, Logau, Rist and Zesen) were members of *Die Fruchtbringende Gesellschaft*, of which mention has already been made. This body, also known from its emblem as *Der Palmenorden*, was in its origin a linguistic rather than a literary society. It was founded just before the Thirty Years War by Prince Ludwig von Anhalt-Cöthen and at its outset was recruited almost exclusively from noblemen; among its early members were two princes and three dukes. In the long run, however, its membership was not solely aristocratic, and many of the participants, who all bore symbolical names such as *Der Nährende* or *Der Schmackhafte*, were commoners in the administrative service of great men. That this influential society should be focused upon courts is a reflection of this aristocratic century. *Die Fruchtbringende Gesellschaft* was a kind of conservation group working in the field of language, seeking to maintain and elevate the standards of German against foreign importation on the one side and popular corruption on the other. About the

54

middle of the century its impetus diminished, and it finally petered out in 1680. But in its hey-day it was a force for linguistic stability in an age of confusion and stress. It was paid plenty of compliments by imitation, for similar societies sprang up in many parts, such as *Die aufrichtige Tannengesellschaft* in Strasbourg in 1633, *Die teutschgesinnte Genossenschaft* in Hamburg in 1643, the Nürnberg *Pegnitzschäfer* in 1644 and *Der Elbschwanorden* also in Hamburg in 1660.

Among the members of *Die Fruchtbringende Gesellschaft* was the Silesian Andreas Gryphius (1616–64), one of the best poets and the outstanding dramatist of the seventeenth century. Almost all Gryphius' poetry is of a sombre cast. The sonnets, which make up a great part of his output, reiterate the motifs of *vanitas vanitatum* and *memento mori*; they portray man ceaselessly beset by disease, assailed by war and cut off by death. Each New Year is for Gryphius an occasion for ostentatious, yet none the less sincere, melancholy. The death of both parents in his boyhood may well have intensified a bent for sombre introspection. His plays, written at a time when theatres were virtually absent from a war-racked Germany, suffer from their remoteness from the living stage. *Cardenio und Celinde* (written 1649, published 1657) takes four figures from Gryphius' own time, entwines them in a mesh of perverted erotic desire, and then displays to them (and to the reader) a solemn moral warning. It is a remarkable play for its time, because it suggests, in spite of verse speech and a ghost, an appreciable element of realism. For the rest, Gryphius' tragedies are static parades, in which the passive virtue of stoicism is foremost; presenting in *Catharina von Georgien* (written *c.* 1646, published 1657) a more than human endurance in a Christian martyr, or in *Carolus Stuardus*, written red-hot in 1649, the mental suffering of a martyred king, Charles I. Gryphius also tried his hand at comedy, adapting the farce of Bottom and Peter Quince in *Peter Squentz* (1658) and achieving a rumbustious success in a comedy of boastful yet cowardly officers, *Horribilicribrifax* (1663).

Social and political conditions in Germany, in contrast to France, were not conducive to a living drama. The one suc-

55

cessful tradition of the theatre in the seventeenth century flourished in schools and at the Viennese court. This was the Jesuit drama, consisting chiefly of plays written in Latin. As most of the audience could not understand the words, a summary was printed for their benefit. And since the words were largely lost, the Jesuit drama concentrated on the eye, on spectacular staging and on the musical ear, evolving more and more towards opera.

So the Jesuit drama did not answer the theatrical needs of the German dramatist, and Gryphius' successor, Daniel Casper von Lohenstein (1635–83), therefore also stood in a kind of theatrical vacuum. His six tragedies resemble those of Gryphius in their insistence on stoical endurance of pain and steadfastness in defeat. The savage atrocities and tortures which in Lohenstein's *Epicharis* (1665) are inflicted on the stage exceed anything Gryphius wrote, except perhaps for his *description* of the protracted death of the heroine in *Catharina von Georgien*. And Lohenstein's plays are written in an inflated, pompous rhetoric (*Schwulst* or 'bombast'), which was long regarded as typical of Baroque writing, but is in reality an extreme form, indeed almost a caricature of it.

Lohenstein, who like Gryphius was a Silesian, and was also a busy administrator for whom literature was a leisure occupation, wrote no plays after he was thirty-eight, turning instead to the novel. He wrote only one, a substantial affair in two volumes, which were published posthumously in 1689. This novel, *Grossmütiger Feldherr Arminius*, is both a patriotic work (it is set at the time of the first serious conflict between the Germanic peoples and the Romans in A.D. 9) and a book full of learned and informative digressions.

Lohenstein's *Arminius* is typical of one side of the aristocratic novel. It is reading matter for the governing nobility and for the extensive body of commoner civil servants who made its government effective. So high was the esteem in which such works were held that a ruling prince did not disdain to appear in print as their author. Among the 'courtly novels' (*höfische Romane*) of the second half of the seventeenth century were two by Duke Anton Ulrich of Brunswick (1633–1714), who from 1704 to his death was the reigning duke.

56

Anton Ulrich wrote two novels, *Die Durchleuchtige Syrerin Armena* in five volumes (1669–73) and *Die römische Octavia* in six (1677–1707). These voluminous works set in motion large numbers of characters, who are systematically graded in a social pattern, and the novels themselves present a model of Anton Ulrich's conception of absolute government.

A novel more obviously designed for entertainment is *Die asiatische Banise* (1689) by a Saxon squire, Heinrich Anselm von Ziegler und Kliphausen (1663–96). This love story, at the end of which the two principal characters live happily ever after, offers an exotic setting, disguises, rescues in the nick of time, and lavish descriptions of slaughter, atrocities and torture, all recounted in the fashionable, ornate and hyperbolical style of the Baroque.

In strong contrast to these extravagant and artificial productions, which appealed to an upper stratum of a hierarchical society and gratified a taste which was soon to disappear, *Der abenteuerliche Simplicissimus* (1669) stands out not only as the best novel but as the finest German work of literature in the whole century. Its author, Hans Jakob Christoffel von Grimmelshausen (*c.* 1622–76), had years of first-hand experience of the Thirty Years War and then, after the peace (1648), spent most of his life as an innkeeper and mayor of a small town in south-west Germany. Grimmelshausen knew what he was writing about and wrote with such freshness and conviction that he has deceived many people into taking his story as autobiography. In *Der abenteuerliche Simplicissimus* the simple-minded hero early experiences the horrors of war, finds himself perforce a soldier and, quitting his naïvety, takes part in battles and skirmishes with uninhibited gusto. The war ends and for a time he becomes an adventurer; but he eventually undergoes a religious conversion, is wrecked on a desert island and is content to remain there in devout meditation. Grimmelshausen writes easily and straight from the shoulder. His fertile imagination is matched by his homely, spontaneous style, and he endows his hero with a spirit of comedy which keeps him on an even keel, come what may. This novel, which is the most balanced work of the age, has none of the affectations and attitudinising of the aristocratic courtly novel, and it shows the potential strength of the popular tradition, to which the folk-songs, hymns and *Volksbücher* also belonged. Grimmelshausen wrote other novels, including one about the adventuress Courasche (who three centuries later appears with Brecht as Mutter Courage), but, humorous and robust as they are, to the point of obscenity, none of these can hold a candle to *Simplicissimus.*

Grimmelshausen's great book did not stand alone as an isolated achievement of the unfashionable but persistent tradition. Some twenty-five years before *Der abenteuerliche Simplicissimus*, Hans Michael Moscherosch (1601–69), an Alsatian magistrate, had published a work which started life as a translation from the Spanish of Francisco Quevedo (1580–1634) and then developed an independent existence as *Wunderbarliche und wahrhaftige Gesichte Philanders von Sittewalt* (1640–3). It is a satire in vivid homely language, a critical mirror of the Germany of that day, a lament for the perversion of indigenous virtues and a denunciation of foreign habits and standards. Christian Weise (1642–1708), a generation younger than Grimmelshausen, also developed a popular style in a cycle of satirical novels, *Die drei Hauptverderber in Deutschland* (1671), *Die drei ärgesten Erznarren in der ganzen Welt* (1672) and *Die drei klügsten Leute in der ganzen Welt* (1675).

Satirical distortion behind a screen of apparent veracity marks the homely prose satire of Christian Reuter (1665–*c.* 1712), whose *Schelmuffskys wahrhaftige und sehr gefährliche Reisebeschreibung* (1696) slyly mocks the reader and simultaneously ridicules the author's former landlady, against whom he conducted a pertinacious and rather unworthy campaign in print. The wild student settled down to respectable life in Berlin before he was thirty and wrote nothing of importance after the conscious absurdity of *Schelmuffsky*, which has a robust realism belonging to the popular tradition.

Something of Grimmelshausen's manner recurs in the work of Johann Beer (1653–1700), who concealed his identity so successfully behind pseudonyms that his authorship of some twenty racy, well-told novels (of which *Der Simplicianische Welt–Kucker*, 1677–9, is a characteristic title) was only discovered in this century. A born story-teller, Beer was also a master of direct, pithy style and of realistic vision.

Perhaps the most intriguing and characteristic figure towards the end of the century is the Augustinian friar Abraham a Sancta Clara (1644–1709), whose original name was Johann Ulrich Megerle. Abraham was a much sought after preacher, who knew how to appeal to the common people and at the same time stood in high favour with the Imperial court. His language, compounded of proverbs, familiar sayings and puns, was put together with the extravagant exuberance of the Baroque. In spite of the ebullience of his style, he was a serious moralist, reproaching the age with its folly and sinfulness in tracts such as *Merk's, Wien* (1680) and *Auf, auf, ihr Christen* (1683).

The seventeenth century shows itself as an age of disparities, an age in which the dominant aristocratic outlook, constantly threatening to freeze in an extravagant gesture, fails to overpower the popular tradition of the preceding period. The century of the full-bottomed wig, which represents an irrepressible desire for affected self-magnification, exaggerated dignity and disguise of the self, was also the age of frankly brutal war and devastating pestilence and want. Vulgar obscenity and pastoral erotic posturing coexisted, and the towering accumulations of *Schwulst* were countered by the direct racy speech of Grimmelshausen and Beer. For all the rigidity in the stylised aristocratic outlook, the seventeenth century is not so much an age with a clearly pronounced character as an age in flux, searching for its identity.

5 Reason and Sentiment: 1700–1770

1. A New Philosophy and a New Piety: 1700–1750

The eighteenth century is often called the age of reason or enlightenment. Yet such generalisations, useful though they can be, always oversimplify and therefore distort. And the eighteenth century, as soon as we take more than a cursory look at it, proves to be an age of sentiment as well as of reason. Reason, enthroned by Descartes, lived side by side with its apparent opposite, sentiment, which was at first evident as the religious expression of a minority.

The roots of the new sentiment go back well into the seventeenth century, just as reason goes back to Descartes. The grandiose oratorical manner of the Baroque divines had outlived itself, and a new emphasis on personal feeling and intimate communion made itself felt in the Church. Two notable personalities fostered the new devout and fervent religious outlook which came to be called 'pietism'. Philipp Jakob Spener (1635–1705), an Alsatian pastor who was later active in Dresden, preached a practical Christianity based on the Bible, in which the exercise of charity was linked with a close personal relationship to God. His views were expressed in an influential book, *Pia Desideria oder herzliches Verlangen nach gottgefälliger Besserung der wahren evangelischen Kirche* (1675). Many families and many individuals reshaped their lives in accordance with Spener's new Christianity of the heart, and writers as different as Klopstock, Wieland and Goethe were at one time or another touched by its sincerity and simplicity.

Spener personally influenced Gottfried Arnold (1666–1714), who was for a short time a professor at Giessen University, but was persecuted because of his religious unorthodoxy and had to leave his appointment. Arnold's self-imposed task was to renew the lost spirit of early Christianity. His *Unparteiische Kirchen- und Ketzerhistorie* (1699–1715), which is based on the view that it is the heretics, as innovators, who have given life to the Church, influenced religious thinking and feeling for a century at least.

Pietistic Christianity also influenced the early life of Christian Thomasius (1655–1728), who was first a lecturer at Leipzig and then a professor at Halle University. The make-up of Thomasius' mind had a touch of mysticism, but this was accompanied by clear-sighted common sense and skill in logical thought, so that in him rationalism of the mind and piety of the heart were combined. Thomasius' works, which are mainly philosophical and juristic, are no longer read, but his influence as a teacher was considerable, and he still stands out for three personal achievements. He fought long and successfully against witch trials and burnings, completing the work begun by Friedrich von Spee.[1] He broke through the tradition that university lectures must be delivered in Latin, giving the first course in German in 1687. And he published the first literary periodical in Germany of a type which, on the English model of the *Spectator*, was to become popular in the early eighteenth century.

The tide of rationalism flowed more strongly and more visibly than the drift of piety. Descartes and Leibniz gave it force, and at the beginning of the eighteenth century it percolated to most sections of the literate public. Gottfried Wilhelm Leibniz (1646–1716), a Hanoverian, was an outstanding mathematician and an ingenious philosopher, who made an influential attempt to resolve the dualism of matter and spirit and communicated an optimistic tone to the arguments of rationalism. Since Leibniz, however, wrote in Latin or French, few people read him, and his doctrines reached the public in a distorted form in the work of Christian Wolff (1679–1754), a professor of Halle University, or in a handbook written by J. C. Gottsched.[2] Wolff's philosophy was set out in a series of volumes appropriately entitled *Vernünftige Gedanken* (1719–23) and Gottsched provided the same matter in handier form

[1] See above, p. 50.   [2] See below, p. 63.

in his *Erste Gründe der gesamten Weltweisheit* (1734).

The new rationalism invaded all forms of literature, even poetry. A Hamburger, Barthold Hinrich Brockes (1680–1747), devoted his patrician leisure hours to composing poetry to demonstrate the glory of God by describing His handiwork. Brockes' plan was a rationalistic one, but his execution of it in the nine volumes of *Irdisches Vergnügen in Gott* (1721–48), which contain his poems, is strikingly original. Conventional presentation of reality is abandoned, and Brockes makes the effort to describe visible things, a planet, a shower of rain or a snowflake, in their detailed reality. Moreover he calls in the other senses, seeking to convey hearing and touch in his poetry. A young Swiss doctor, Albrecht von Haller (1708–77), who later became the foremost medical authority of the age, broke new ground in 1728 by venturing into the Alps for pleasure and interest. Shortly afterwards he wrote an impressive descriptive poem, contrasting the simplicity of rural alpine existence with the corruption of city life. *Die Alpen* (1732) is one of the first works to idealise scenic nature and to exalt the untaught natural man. The emotion which Haller could only partly express because of his decorous, reticent temperament pours out in the poems of Johann Christian Günther (1695–1723), whose life went awry because he could not inhibit feeling. Günther's personal experiences emerge in his poetry, often unaltered and unidealised, so that, just as Haller anticipates Rousseau's admiration for uncivilised man, Günther for his part looks forward to Goethe's early poetry.

All these poets were in some degree heirs to the style of the seventeenth century, using elaborate combinations of standardised phrases and images, though each of them had something new to offer. A transformation in German poetic style came first, not in the serious poetry of the age, but in slight and trivial productions. Friedrich von Hagedorn (1708–54), a comfortably situated Hamburger and one-time diplomat, wrote many poems as the occupation of his leisure hours. They make no pretension to originality or profundity, but they are phrased with a deft elegance which was new to German literature. The so-called Anacreontic poets, too, Johann Nikolaus Götz (1721–81) and Johann Peter Uz (1719–1803), wrote conventional poems in praise of wine, women and song, matching the lightness of their style to the slenderness of their matter. Johann Wilhelm Ludwig Gleim (1719–1803), for many years secretary to the cathedral chapter at Halberstadt, wrote similar make-believe love poetry, though he was also touched by the rising patriotism which the victories of Frederick II of Prussia were beginning to arouse, writing a volume of war poetry, *Preussische Kriegslieder* (1758).

The stream of novels which had poured out in the second half of the seventeenth century ran dry at the beginning of the eighteenth, perhaps because the new rationalism made people unwilling to accept their extravagances. Only one novel of note appeared in the first forty years of the new century. *Die Insel Felsenburg* (as it is now known – the original title was much longer) was published in four volumes between 1731 and 1743. Its author, Johann Gottfried Schnabel (1692–1752), who wrote nothing else of importance, managed in this novel to provide something for everyone; he not only combined the pietism and rationalism of the age, but catered for a taste for adventure and a liking for erotic diversions.

Meanwhile the poets had been feeling their way; Brockes and Haller, Uz and Gleim groped tentatively towards new means of expression. Then, in the fourth decade of the century, came a determined attempt to reform all German literature in accordance with rational principles, and this meant – standardisation. Johann Christian Gottsched (1700–66) was the man who conceived this bold and somewhat daunting plan. Gottsched was a man of ambition and energy, with a developed sense for organisation. He had settled in Leipzig and been appointed a professor at the university there, and now he embarked on his campaign for the renovation and rationalisation of German literature. Gottsched, whose programme was set out in *Eine critische Dichtkunst für die Deutschen* (1730), recommended the adoption of French literary principles and canons of taste and – as a means to that end – the imitation of French poems and plays. He assumed that German literature, if it was to equal the French, would have to develop along similar lines. His aim was patriotic, and he paradoxically urged imitation of the French because he wished for a flourish-

ing German literature. His plan ignored the differing conditions prevailing in the two countries, the metropolitan
centralisation of France and the parochial fragmentation of
Germany; but it would be unjust to reproach Gottsched with
this misapprehension, for the modern awareness of environ-
mental forces was only to emerge, with Herder, in the next
generation.

At first Gottsched seemed to carry all before him. Seconded
by his gifted wife and by the able theatre directress Frau
Neuber, and surrounded by a swarm of disciples, he imposed
his will and amassed a number of model works, chiefly
tragedies in the French manner. But in the following decade
the tide began to turn against him. The inseparable Swiss
critics Johann Jakob Bodmer (1698–1783) and Johann Jakob
Breitinger (1701–76) took up the cause of imagination, as-
serting a place in literature for *das Wunderbare* in their
manifestos, Bodmer's *Critische Abhandlung von dem Wun-
derbaren in der Poesie* (1740) and Breitinger's *Critische
Dichtkunst*, the very title of which was a challenge to Gottsched. The dispute between the two parties now seems trivial,
for they were in agreement over large areas, and the Swiss
defence of imagination was timid enough. What mattered was
that they succeeded in weakening the authority of Gottsched,
whose inelastic views were not adequate to guide a new age.

While these pugnacious theorists fought their wordy battle,
a mild little man, a professorial colleague of Gottsched, made
a name for himself by poems, comedies and a novel. Christian
Fürchtegott Gellert (1715–69) was not a particularly distinguished writer, but his sensitive temperament caught the exact
mixture of reason, sentiment and moral feeling which appealed to the readers of the seventeen-forties. Morality was the
central theme. Gellert's popular verse fables carry heavily
stressed morals, his comedies (such as *Die Betschwester*, 1745)
are moral satires, and his novel, *Das Leben der schwedischen
Gräfin von G ...* (1747–8), is a counterpoint of rational pro-
priety and passionate misbehaviour. Gellert also conducted a
vast moral correspondence with those who brought to him
their moral and emotional problems. His amiable and well-
intentioned writings won, surprisingly, a kind word from

Frederick the Great, who otherwise neither understood nor esteemed German literature.

2. A European Literature

The accustomed patterns and routine techniques of the first half of the century were suddenly set at nought by a new work, part of which appeared in 1748 in the *Bremer Beiträge*, a series published by defectors from Gottsched's camp. This new work was a Christian epic, *Der Messias* by Friedrich Gottlob Klopstock (1724–1803). Klopstock, who was to enjoy for most of his life a poet's pension, had read *Paradise Lost* while at school, responding to it with enthusiasm and determining to write a German poem of equivalent inspiration and scale. The first three cantos of *Der Messias* steadily spread Klopstock's fame, helped by enthusiastic propaganda from Bodmer. The epic, which was completed in 1773, was written in 'Homeric' hexameters and was the first major work in German to dispense with rhyme. Its theme is the Passion and, in the Homeric manner, the action is conducted on a celestial plane (angels of light versus fallen angels) as well as on the earthly scene. The popularity of *Der Messias* was partly religious and partly patriotic, for the emergence of an original work on the largest scale executed by a German was a heartening spectacle. The poem now seems rather faded, for the emotional pitch is too high and the action too slow to hold the interest through so long a work. Klopstock's odes, on the other hand, written on a monumental scale with powerful, imaginative use of language, are poems of compelling grandeur. Their collected publication in 1771 gave Klopstock's work a strong formative influence through the 1770s.

Klopstock was not primarily a poet of nature, for he was dominated rather by the grandeur of God and the magnitude of the human spirit made in the image of God. The feeling for nature in poetry was cultivated and developed in the middle of the century by two poets, one older and one younger than Klopstock. Ewald von Kleist (1715–59), a close friend of Lessing and an upright gentleman who died of wounds as a

c

Prussian major after the battle of Kunersdorf, admired English literature and was particularly taken with James Thomson's *The Seasons*. His poem *Der Frühling* (1748), written in hexameters, is nevertheless an independent work, tingeing the contemplation of nature with a melancholy which is Kleist's own. When war came in 1756, Kleist, who was deeply moved by love for his country, shifted the focus of his poetry from nature to patriotism, writing an ode 'An die preussische Armee' (1757) and a short blank-verse epic on an ancient Greek subject, *Cissides und Paches* (1758), which celebrates soldierly comradeship and exalts death suffered for one's country.

The younger poet of nature was in one sense not a poet at all, for he wrote in prose. Salomon Gessner (1730–88), who was a minor artist as well as a writer, imbued his pastoral idylls (*Idyllen*, 1756) with a delicate poetic atmosphere, conjuring up a serene undisturbed countryside, cultivated and unalarming. It is an unreal Arcadian world, which appealed to an urban public increasingly aware of its separation from nature.

The giants of the middle of the century, dwarfing these lesser figures, were Winckelmann and Lessing, the new discoverer of ancient art and the man who put German literature on the European map. Johann Joachim Winckelmann (1717–68), one of the few men of letters to die by murder, was a Prussian of the humblest origin, who pursued learning, especially Greek and Latin, with single-minded enthusiasm and monomanic passion. He spent his best years in Rome and Naples examining antique sculpture and developing his conception of the noble simplicity and grandeur of Greek art. Even before he went south he set out his ideas clearly in *Gedanken über die Nachahmung der griechischen Werke in der Malerei und Bildhauerkunst* (1755), which his great work, *Geschichte der Kunst des Altertums* (1764) amplifies with authoritative erudition. It was he who gave to the eighteenth century a new classical horizon.

Gotthold Ephraim Lessing (1729–81) had all the best qualities of the *Aufklärung* or enlightenment, sharp intellect, rational clarity and spotless integrity; but he had also qualities

66

of perception and empathy which transcend the *Aufklärung* and made him, however unwillingly, the pioneer for a new generation of poets and dramatists in the 1770s. Lessing began as a playwright and from time to time returned to writing plays. After modest early comedies he wrote the first German domestic tragedy, *Miss Sara Sampson* (1755) and some years later produced a lively, alert and highly topical comedy in *Minna von Barnhelm* (1767). *Emilia Galotti* (1772) represented a more mature and convincing domestic tragedy (*bürgerliches Trauerspiel*), which developed a vein of social criticism, and *Nathan der Weise* (1779), with its noble plea for tolerance, revealed the potentiality of poetic humanitarian drama. Lessing's critical work was astringent, sometimes even harsh, but it was always penetrating and always insisted on the highest standards of literary integrity, whether in the contemporary criticism of the *Literaturbriefe* (1759–65) or in the Aristotelian discussions of *Die Hamburgische Dramaturgie* (1767–9). *Laokoon*, taking a statement by Winckelmann as its starting-point, took a sharp look at critical confusions and established valid points of distinction between the poetic and plastic arts. And his religious polemics and constructive writings (which include *Nathan der Weise* and *Die Erziehung des Menschengeschlechts*, 1780) testify to a sense of reverence as well as to a love of truth. Lessing was more feared than loved, but the very rigour with which he discussed German literature was the highest compliment he could pay it. He made no allowances, and what stood up to his scrutiny could maintain itself as European as well as German.

Wieland, a much milder man, also had horizons which extended beyond Germany. Christoph Martin Wieland (1733–1813) was first a town clerk in his native Swabian Biberach and then a tutor of princes at Weimar. Quickly pensioned, he lived on there as a respected man of letters. At first a protégé of Bodmer, writing religious epics and indulging in sentimental ecstasies, Wieland swung away in the 1770s to exotic verse tales in the French manner and to rationalistic novels such as the mildly satirical *Don Sylvio von Rosalva* (1764) and the philosophical *Agathon* (1766), a manifesto of the golden mean. *Der goldene Spiegel* (1772), a fantasy on political education, won Wieland his call to Weimar, and *Die Abderiten* satirised obscurantism and narrow-mindedness. Wieland also wrote an attractive verse romance, *Oberon* (1780), and made the first translation of a collection of Shakespeare's plays, twenty-one in prose and *A Midsummer Night's Dream* in verse (1762–6). He was versatile, sensitive, flexible and easygoing, and he communicated these qualities to his writing, proving that German letters were capable of elegance and precision, of urbanity and civilised playfulness. His journal *Der teutsche Merkur* (1773–1810) was an important factor in German intellectual life, especially in its first twenty years.

Both Lessing and Wieland represented in different ways what was best in the *Aufklärung*, though Lessing also reached beyond it towards the dynamism of the *Sturm und Drang*, and Wieland to some extent anticipated both classicism and romanticism. Very different was the man who could see no further than the *Aufklärung* and its rationalism. Friedrich Nicolai (1733–1811) had in his twenties been in the forefront of literature, but from his late thirties on he was a fussy and obstinate opponent of change. Nicolai, who had once been Lessing's friend and a contributor to the *Literaturbriefe*, declined into a figure of ridicule for the *Sturm und Drang*, the classicists and the romantics. The reputation of Karl Wilhelm Ramler (1725–98) also waned, but Ramler abstained from foolish polemic and, furthermore, achieved some poetry of merit within the narrow limits of an austere classicism.

According to personal taste and prejudice the *Aufklärung* can be seen as an age of pedantry, complacency and self-important triviality, or as a phase in the organisation of the human intellect, in the rejection of bigotry and the fostering of laudable ideals of freedom and tolerance. Like all movements it had its conspicuous peaks and its obscure recesses and all have to be considered in a balanced view. A complex intellectual climate prevailed over Europe, and German literature, participating in the climatic shift, became itself European. Individuals made what they could of the new possibilities according to their capabilities, ranging from the achievement of Lessing, through the competence of Wieland to the maunderings of Nicolai.

The *Aufklärung* was more an attitude of mind than a move
ment. It lasted longer than the eighteenth century, beginning
in the late seventeenth and leaving a recognisable wake in the
early nineteenth. Heine's *Harzreise*, for instance, contains an
unmistakable straggler of 'enlightenment'. The *Aufklärung*
thus persisted just because it could survive as an attitude when
it ceased to be a movement. Its dynamic phase covers only
some forty years, say, 1730–70. For all the humanitarianism
these were years of frequent wars; but the Wars of the Austrian Succession in the 1740s and the Seven Years War (1756–
63), though they brought harrowing suffering and want to
many, were not universal catastrophes like the great war of the
previous century. The *Aufklärung* ideal of freedom was sel-
dom realised, for it was bred in the hey-day of despotism, yet
the rational and benevolent philosophy of the age turned
many princes into *enlightened* despots. Meanwhile aristocratic
patronage, though still important, was declining, and the
middle class was on the rise as well as on the make; and though
the lack of a metropolis made for a certain parochialism, men
like Lessing, Winckelmann and Wieland proved that it could
be overcome.

6 The Great Age: 1770–1800

1. *Wave of Protest: 1770–1780*

The current of faith and feeling, partly obscured in the early part of the century, had never ceased to flow. Klopstock had triumphantly vindicated reverence and love and friendship, Lessing had allowed sentiment in *Miss Sara Sampson*, and Haller, Salomon Gessner and Ewald von Kleist had given expression to genuine emotion. But all of them, even Klopstock, the most original, had written in conformity with habits of thought and a discipline of style which belonged at least in part to rationalism. Up to 1770 successive generations had sufficient common ground to understand each other. In the following decade this ceased to be true. A mighty stirring took place over the whole intellectual life of Germany, and at two conspicuous geographical points (on the middle Rhine and in Göttingen), it flared or blossomed into a short-lived spell of intense original creativity.

The first signs of this wind of change had appeared sporadically in the previous decade. Johann Georg Hamann (1730–88), a man whose alternations of irresistible impulse and harrowing remorse foreshadowed the emotional life of the next generation, published in *Sokratische Denkwürdigkeiten* (1759) a defence of genius and a justification of inspiration, both psychological realities to which the first half of the century had paid only lip-service. Barely noticed at the time, this work was the first step towards the *Sturm und Drang*, as the new age of ferment was later to be called.

More fruitful and far-reaching impulses came from Johann Gottfried Herder (1744–1803), a young theologian from East Prussia, who possessed the most fertile theoretical brain of the new generation. Taking, like Rousseau, whom he admired, the side of Nature against art and letters, he condemned the elaborate and sophisticated writing of his own time and turned back to simple folk-song and to what he believed to be folk-type literature on a grand scale, to Homer, Ossian, Shakespeare and the Bible. He collected folk-songs and published them in *Volkslieder* in 1778. But before this he had established a reputation with *Fragmente über die neuere deutsche Literatur* (1767), in which the great idea of his life, the conception of organic growth in history, according to which states, languages, literatures and institutions have their youth, their prime and their decline, was already manifest, standing in sharp contrast to the belief in steady and continuous progress held by the rationalists. Herder's symposium *Von deutscher Art and Kunst* (1773), in which Goethe participated, exalted Shakespeare, Ossian, folk-song and Gothic architecture. Herder further developed his evolutionary historical ideas in original and learned treatises, especially the *Älteste Urkunde des Menschengeschlechts* (1774–6) and the *Ideen zur Philosophie der Geschichte der Menschheit* (1784–91). In addition, his personal influence, especially on Goethe in Strasburg in 1770 and to some extent later in Weimar, was considerable. And the repercussions of his rethinking of history are still felt by us today.

In the year in which Herder's *Fragmente* appeared, there was published a tragedy by Heinrich Wilhelm von Gerstenberg (1737–1823), a former officer in the Danish army. Its title was *Ugolino* and its source was Dante's *Inferno*. In structure it was as concentrated and regular as Gottsched could have wished; but its simple action, the death of Count Ugolino and his three sons by starvation in prison, is harrowing and heartrending in its cumulative intensity. This was a new step into horror with a new depth of emotion. Gerstenberg also drew attention in his *Briefe über die Merkwürdigkeiten der Literatur* (1766) to the genius of Shakespeare (whom Wieland had recently translated) and to his gift for the expression of overpowering feeling.

Gerstenberg may be said to fire the first warning shot for the *Sturm und Drang*. This is a term for the literature of the next decade (1770–80), to which two distinct meanings have

71

ed. In one aspect it denotes a general turbulence
and in the lives particularly of the young over the
of Germany, an awareness of ecstasies and des-
hich the last generation had ignored; and it is on
d applied to a group of young men, centred on
Main (Frankfort) and middle Rhine (Strasburg),
who made a cult of genius, expressed in eccentricity, enthusiasm, passion and despair. The soul of this coterie was
Goethe, then in his early twenties. Johann Wolfgang Goethe
(1749–1832) had quickly tired of the poetry and plays which
his elders favoured, had passed through a phase of cynicism
at Leipzig University, and then in 1770 found himself quite
suddenly as a lyric poet and a 'genius'. A love affair (with
Friederike Brion) and some months spent with Herder at
Strasburg were the outward causes of this change, but the
dynamism came from something within Goethe himself, which
was now suddenly released. The word *Genie* ('genius'), which
had been nurtured by Young,[1] fostered by Hamann and
tended by Herder, came into prominence in this generation
signifying, not something one could have but something one
was. The genius was an original personality, and whether or
not he could write or paint, he had to act according to his own
laws in disregard of accepted patterns and conventions. Such
an original genius was what Goethe now became. He wrote
poems of wonderful tenderness and power, but he also went
for midnight rides and clambered about on the precarious
stonework high up on Strasburg Minster. In the years which
followed he wrote a vital and angry play of a great man
brought low by plotting, base intriguers. This tragedy, *Götz
von Berlichingen* (1773), split into a multitude of short scenes,
was Goethe's response to Shakespeare. He wrote dynamic
poems of revolt like 'Prometheus' and a novel of obsessive love
and suicidal introversion, *Die Leiden des jungen Werthers*
(1774). *Werther* quickly conquered not only Germany but the
civilised world (Napoleon, surprisingly, read it seven times).
Simultaneously Goethe began a play on Faust, the seeker after
knowledge, which turned into a love tragedy of Faust and the

[1] Edward Young (1683–1765), author of *Night Thoughts* and *Con-
jectures on Original Composition*.

girl Gretchen – a play which Goethe was unable to finish to his satisfaction, so that it remained for the time being unpublished.

While Goethe was writing these works, he was living a full, energetic and boisterous social life with a number of cronies of his own age. These men are the principal figures of the *Sturm und Drang*. Johann Michael Reinhold Lenz (1751–92), an East German from the Baltic provinces, who possessed a vivid talent and an unstable personality, had a brief summer in Goethe's sunshine before returning east to be picked up dead one night in a Moscow street. His eccentric but realistic play *Der Hofmeister* (1774) was surpassed by an extraordinarily powerful social tragedy, *Die Soldaten* (1776), dealing with military life in its relationship to the civilian population. Heinrich Leopold Wagner (1747–79) wrote two plays, one of which (*Die Kindermörderin*, 1776) was an impressive representation of the theme of the girl seduced by an officer and turning to infanticide. Friedrich Maximilian Klinger (1752–1831), an orphan whom Goethe helped financially, wrote a best-selling tragedy of intense fratricidal passion (*Die Zwillinge*, 1776) as well as other works in which *Genies* are the principal characters. Klinger, after hard years, made his way and finished up as a Russian general. Another poor boy of talent, Friedrich ('Maler') Müller (1749–1825), wrote semi-realistic rural idylls (*Die Schafschur*, 1775, and *Das Nusskernen*, 1776) as well as a play on Faust, *Fausts Leben dramatisiert* (1778). Müller's genius, both as painter and writer, proved to have shallow roots, and in his later years he maintained himself in Rome by acting as a guide to German visitors.

The explosion of genius quickly spent itself, as all explosions must, and the first to realise this was the earliest and most original of all, Goethe, who in 1775 accepted an invitation to the Weimar court, turning his back on his roistering companions and quickly changing his way of life. Left to themselves, the other geniuses of Frankfort and Strasburg soon burned themselves out or subsided into normal life.

Simultaneously, many miles to the north and quite without direct link, another cohesive demonstration of youth took

73

place. The participants were chiefly students of Göttingen University, who one fine September night in 1772 danced round a forest oak in the moonlight and declared themselves a German league. This is the origin of the *Göttinger Hain* or *Hainbund*, which differed from the Rhine–Main group in its predilection for melancholy against the mid-German vociferous energy. The *Hain* was primarily lyrical, the Frankfort *Sturm und Drang* dramatic. Yet at one point the two groups touched. Joseph Anton Leisewitz (1752–1806), a sensitive and hypochondriac civil servant, who was a Hain member, ventured to write a play, *Julius von Tarent* (1776), an embodiment of fraternal strife, which was one of the outstanding successes of the age. He submitted it for a competition, in which Klinger's *Die Zwillinge* was also a candidate. Klinger won, and Leisewitz never wrote another play. For the rest, the Göttingen students were mostly lyric poets. The finest of them was Ludwig Christoph Heinrich Hölty (1748–76), a sensitive yet simple nature, who wrote so insistently on the brief happiness of May and on young love denied fulfilment that it seems a premonition of his early death from tuberculosis. The two brothers Stolberg, Count Christian (1748–1821) and Count Friedrich Leopold (1750–1819) supplemented their often amateurish lyric poetry with the antics of supposed genius. And Johann Martin Miller (1750–1814) composed sentimental rural poetry, and also wrote one of the most successful novels of that generation, *Siegwart* (1776), a story of contrasted happy and unhappy loves, rich in atmosphere and robust in narration.

Away from these compact groups a few others wrote in fresh and original tones. Gottfried August Bürger (1747–94), who allowed his private life to get into an inextricable tangle, stood close to the Hain without actually being a member. His outstanding achievement is the popular ballad 'Lenore' (1773), which became famous for its galloping rhythm, onomatopoeic interjections and macabre story-telling. Matthias Claudius (1740–1815) of Wandsbeck near Hamburg was a poet of simple integrity and realistic triviality, who also practised popular journalism in his one-man periodical *Der Wandsbecker Bote* (1770–5). More related to the dynamism of

74

Goethe and Klinger is the powerful, sensual, undisciplined novel *Ardinghello* (1787) by Johann Jakob Wilhelm Heinse (1746–1803). And in the far south the Württemberger Christian Daniel Schubart (1739–91) fulminated against princes until he was kidnapped and imprisoned in 1777. Simultaneously a scattering of sentimental novels of various modes and tones appeared, of which the best-known is perhaps the *Geschichte des Fräuleins von Sternheim* (1771) by Sophie von La Roche (1731–1807), whom Wieland had once loved.

If the occurrence of *Sturm und Drang* writing was curiously sporadic, the *Sturm und Drang* public seems to have been widely and well distributed. A change of mind and heart now began which, in its completion some twenty years later, was to earn the term 'romantic'. A lapse of time was necessary, for the *Sturm und Drang*, though its romantic implications are now clear to us, came before the world was ready for it. It was perhaps a misfortune for the movement that it came at a moment when the political situation in Europe had stabilised itself after the suffering and destruction of the Seven Years War. The system of despotism, enlightened or otherwise, seemed secure, and the only struggle for freedom was the remote revolt of the American colonists.

2. Goethe after 1775

The wide span of Goethe's life and his exceptional stature make it convenient to consider his life and work from this point in a section by itself. Up to 1775 he was something of a pack leader, but after his arrival in Weimar he ploughed his own furrow, seeking no disciples, though ready for intellectual discussion with Herder and later on cultivating a regular interchange of ideas with Schiller. His solitude was not that of the recluse; he was the self-sufficient man of character, exploring life with energy, curiosity and independence.

After the effervescence and turmoil of the Strasburg, Wetzlar and Frankfort years Goethe was translated in Weimar to a circle of aristocratic decorum and to a world of practical affairs. From being the Duke's favourite he became his right-hand man, and for some years he was chief administrator of the Duchy. The time that was taken for business was lost for poetry. From 1775 to 1786 Goethe wrote some dozens of poems and versions of two plays (*Egmont* and *Iphigenie*) and of a novel (*Wilhelm Meisters theatralische Sendung*), but these larger works did not attain a sufficiently conclusive form to merit publication. Meanwhile Goethe's personality ripened, all the more so because he was in close contact with Frau von Stein, a woman of rare breeding and civilised temper. In the mid-1780s a new ideal began to dominate him. A growing impatience with German letters and conditions of life was complemented by a quickening admiration for the classicism of Greece and Rome. In 1786 he set out with precipitate haste for Italy, where he remained for almost two years. In Italy, in warmth and luminous sunshine and far from routine drudgery, the springs of creative work were released anew. During or immediately after his Italian journey he completed *Egmont, Iphigenie auf Tauris* (both 1787) and *Torquato Tasso* (1790), three plays concerned respectively with the dynamic individual, the influence of the humane personality, and the conflict between civilised society and extreme individualism in the artist. He virtually abandoned his early Faust play, publishing it in truncated form as *Faust, Ein Fragment* (1790), and a few years later he completed *Wilhelm Meisters Lehrjahre* (1795), a fascinating study in the development of character. These works herald a phase of classicism, though all of them had germinated at an earlier stage.

From this point, for some dozen years, Goethe cultivated the Antique, writing in classical verse form (notably the *Römische Elgien*, 1795) and composing an engaging idyllic poem combining pastoral quality and Homeric touches against a background of the French Revolution (*Hermann und Dorothea*, 1796). His collaborator during this phase in his career (1794–1805) was Schiller,[1] and the two men made a determined effort to direct German intellectual life into idealistic channels by classical example. Yet, though Goethe and Schiller experienced a classical period, Germany did not. The two men, for all their earnest advocacy, met with only

[1] See below, p. 78.

slight response. The classical discipline and the stringent standards which were so self-evidently important to them, passed the general public by, and only a few congenial spirits, such as the diplomat and educationalist Wilhelm von Humboldt (1767–1835) lent their support. And so the classicism of Germany in the late eighteenth century is largely an illusion, created by the exceptional stature of its two notable advocates.

In the new century Goethe's formal classicism waned. At the same time he withdrew from political and administrative tasks, devoting himself to science, to his varied collections and to occasional works of literature. *Die Wahlverwandtschaften* (1809) is a concentrated and symmetrical novel, subtly treating problems of personal relationship in marriage. In *Der West-östliche Diwan* (1819) Goethe borrowed from Persian poetry (then highly fashionable) to create a new kind of verse of balance and relaxation. The great literary focus of his later years was *Faust*, on which he worked especially from 1797 to 1806 (*1. Teil*, 1808) and from 1826 to 1831 (*2. Teil*, 1832). *Faust*, which reflects at different points all Goethe's moods and views and all the literary and intellectual currents of his long life-span, presents a wide-ranging commentary on human emotions and human endeavour made from the vantage points of youth, middle and old age and expressed in a work of unique form. *Faust* and the magnificent and original lyric poetry which Goethe poured out so generously all his life with as little apparent effort in age as in youth make up the primary artistic achievement of his long life.

3. The Last Two Decades of the Eighteenth Century

The classicism which Goethe attempted to establish in Germany towards the end of the century received some backing from Johann Heinrich Voss (1751–1826), a schoolmaster in Holstein, who published a notable (and still popular) hexametrical translation of the *Odyssey* in 1781 and supplemented it in 1793 with the *Iliad*. Karl Philipp Moritz (1756–93) also came out as a supporter of Goethean classicism, but he remains chiefly known for a ruthlessly self-analytical and unclassical psychological novel, *Anton Reiser* (1785–90), while Voss moved from the austerely Homeric plane to sentimental, though attractive, idylls in classical verse form with *Luise* and *Der siebzigste Geburtstag*.

The man who was to be Goethe's most gifted and zealous collaborator in the attempt to educate the public to a humane classicism began with works of a crassness and violence which horrified Goethe, then only a few years distant from his own *Sturm und Drang*. Friedrich Schiller (1759–1805), brought up in Württemberg, an intellectual backwater of Germany, wrote three belated *Sturm und Drang* plays, including *Die Räuber* (1781), a brutal tragedy of well-meaning enthusiasm and passionate individualism, and *Kabale und Liebe* (1783), perhaps the most powerful *bürgerliches Trauerspiel* ever written. *Don Carlos* (1787), a historical tragedy of extraordinary eloquence and beauty, indicated a shift from Schiller's original crude harshness; but after it he fell silent.

Appointed a professor at Jena in 1788 and given a handsome pension in 1791, he devoted himself for a time to the philosophy of Kant. Immanuel Kant (1724–1800) stands out as a giant among the German philosophers of the eighteenth century. His penetrating critical analyses, of which the most famous is the *Kritik der reinen Vernunft* (1781), disposed of his predecessors' inconsistencies and established an idealistic philosophy, centred on an autonomous moral world, which aroused immense interest among the educated and gave German philosophical thought its direction for more than a century. Schiller was caught up in the current of Kantian enthusiasm and for a time devoted his energies to a study of aesthetics in the light of Kant's idealism. In a series of essays, in which *Über die ästhetische Erziehung des Menschen in einer Reihe von Briefen* (1795) and *Über naive und sentimentalische Dichtung* (1795–6) especially stand out, he clarified his own ideas and conceived an educational view of art which enabled him to resume creative writing.

Simultaneously Schiller struck up an intellectual friendship with Goethe, discussing in person and exchanging frequent letters between Jena and Weimar. Their correspondence, first published in 1828–9, is indispensable for an understanding of their classical phase. Schiller, like Goethe, wrote poetry in classical measures, and his later plays, written in blank verse, are almost all classical in their balance and restraint and in their noble idealism. The greatest of these later works is the first, the massive so-called trilogy of *Wallenstein* (1799). In reality a vast tragedy in two parts with a prelude, *Wallenstein* shows the brittleness of human grandeur and the weakness which is concealed in those we call great. *Maria Stuart* (1800) is a study in conscience and in the corruption induced by power. *Die Jungfrau von Orleans* (1801) treats in romantic terms a failure to live up to an ideal of dedication and sacrifice, and *Wilhelm Tell* (1804) forsakes tragedy for *Schauspiel* in its presentation of the defence of human rights. From all these *Die Braut von Messina* (1803) differs radically; in the form of a Greek tragedy, complete with chorus, it displays destructive passion expressing itself through Nemesis. It must always be remembered that Schiller's tragedies were above all stage-plays, powerful and effective works by a man who instinctively perceived the needs of the theatre and progressively added to intuition the profit of accumulated experience.

The third great writer of this would-be classical age was even more remote and solitary than Goethe or Schiller, and had much less of the public ear. Friedrich Hölderlin (1770–1843) came from Schiller's homeland and sought and received some help from him. If Goethe and Schiller were deeply convinced of the educative power of the classical ideal, Hölderlin went much farther. Though he knew the greatness of Greece to be past, it remained for him a living, uplifting experience in the present. Much of his poetry is a passionate and beautiful lament for the loss of the Greece which he feels to be his own true homeland. In powerful mythical poems he expresses his own solitude and his moving consciousness of the plight of his fellow-men. Few poets have had a more rapturous vision of the ideal and a more agonising awareness of its distance from reality. Hölderlin's verse moves from the smaller classical forms, through elegiacs ('Brot und Wein' or 'Menons Klagen um Diotima') and hexameters ('Der Archipelagus') to the free rhythms of 'Patmos' or 'Die Friedensfeier'. He wrote in addition a highly subjective novel, *Hyperion* (1797–9), and

79

a profound unfinished tragedy, *Der Tod des Empedokles* (1798).

The educative classicism of Goethe and Schiller and Hölderlin's Greek enthusiasm coincided, paradoxically enough, with the outbreak of the French Revolution in 1789, the Terror and the early conquests of Bonaparte. Here and there these events are obliquely reflected, as in Goethe's *Hermann und Dorothea* or Hölderlin's 'Die Friedensfeier', but classicism for the most part deliberately disregarded the upheavals of the time in the honest belief that the values of humanity could best be safeguarded by a resolute and disciplined devotion to the Greek heritage. No doubt this remoteness from events is a further reason for the failure of classicism to win adherents. The political events which could have given the *Sturm und Drang* a powerful momentum came too late to be of service to it; but they came in time to thwart Goethe's and Schiller's classical aspirations.

7 The Romantic Age: 1800–1830

1. The Romantic Movement

In the hindsight of our present-day perspective the closing years of the eighteenth century seem to be dominated by Goethe and Schiller, pictured perhaps as the familiar double statue of Weimar, where they stand with clasped hands and self-consciously noble gaze. But behind their backs all kinds of books, many of which must have earned their contempt or disapproval, continued to be written. Freiherr Adolf von Knigge (1752–96) capped the *Aufklärung* with his book of social psychology and wise advice on man management, *Über den Umgang mit Menschen* (1788), a bestseller of that generation. The Sterne-like *Reise in die mittäglichen Provinzen von Frankreich* (1791–1805) of Moritz August von Thümmel (1738–1817) kept up an earlier tradition of the whimsical, humorous, sentimental journey. Though Karl Philipp Moritz[1] (1756–93) later became a friend of Goethe, his autobiographical novel *Anton Reiser* (1785–90) had a depth of introspection which Goethe had early discarded. And towards the end of the century a new and original practitioner of the novel of mood, irony and spiritual exaltation appeared in Jean Paul, in private life Johann Paul Richter (1763–1825). A country pastor's son, Jean Paul in his early life suffered want almost to the point of destitution, and then in a single decade wrote a series of novels which quickly brought him fame and financial security. They include four large-scale works, *Hesperus* (1795), *Siebenkäs* (1796–7), *Titan* (1800–3) and *Flegeljahre* (1804–5), and the miniatures *Leben des vergnügten Schulmeisterleins Maria Wuz* (1790) and *Leben des Quintus Fixlein* (1796). These novels and stories, which are constantly pre-

[1] See also above, p. 77.

81

occupied with the gap between aspiration and reality, brim over with eccentric, grotesque humour, effusive sentiment and warm humanity. Highly idiosyncratic amalgams of diverse and apparently contradictory elements, they ramble incoherently, achieving from time to time passages of breathtaking beauty. It is not customary to reckon Jean Paul as a romantic, perhaps because he was not an intimate of the self-styled romantics of the end of the century. But in logical inconsequence, in the primacy of emotion, and in addiction to self-irony, he is certainly what is usually understood as 'romantic', and he undoubtedly bridges the gap between the *Sturm und Drang* and romanticism.

Romantic movements are recorded all over Europe in the first years of the nineteenth century. In England the rural simplicity of Wordsworth, the luxurious imaginings of Keats, the impatient idealism of Shelley and the diabolism of Byron all go to make up a picture of unusual richness. In Germany the creative beginnings are less impressive. The new outlook was first self-consciously propagated by a group of young men centred on Jena University. The brothers Schlegel (both of them, curiously enough, classicists by training) took the lead. Friedrich Schlegel (1772–1829) wrote in *Lucinde* (1799) an eccentric novel containing intimate confessions of illicit love; and by his provocative, paradoxical epigrams, served up as *Fragmente*, he gave the movement a reputation for cerebration rather than emotion. His elder brother August Wilhelm (1767–1845) was a superb translator, who not only began a splendid German version of Shakespeare but also opened up the seemingly romantic world of Spanish literature. Ludwig Tieck, a gifted though easily influenced and facile writer, wrote an extravagant romantic equivalent of *Wilhelm Meister* in *Franz Sternbalds Wanderungen* (1798), which has a sixteenth-century setting. He gave the new movement its characteristic fairy-tale in *Der Blonde Eckbert* (1797) and attempted an encyclopedic example of the fusion of forms in the enormous undramatic drama *Kaiser Octavianus* (1804).

Friedrich von Hardenberg, a young nobleman who wrote under the pseudonym Novalis (1772–1801), was the most

original of these early romantics, combining an intense introspective life with the practical discharge of his duties as an
inspector of mines. The death of his fiancée, a sixteen-year-
old girl, projected him into a phase of despair, which he resolved in a religious experience; the reflection of this crisis
is seen in the partly prose and partly verse *Hymnen an die
Nacht* (1797). Some of these hymns express with frightening
intensity the death-wish which is the ultimate romantic vision.
Novalis also wrote hymns for use in church and created in the
'blue flower' (*die blaue Blume*) of his unfinished novel *Heinrich von Ofterdingen* the typical symbol of romantic longing.
And he cherished a historical vision of a beautiful idealised
medieval world, compounded of courtly civilisation and refined mysticism, a Christendom purged of selfish ambition,
territorial aggrandisement and economic motive.

The first wave of romanticism, led by the Schlegels and
Tieck and reaching its finest embodiment in Novalis, shared
with classicism, with which its authors had personal and intellectual affinities, an idealism which was remote from the
clashes of politics and the sordid egotism of trade. The historic
events of the time could not be for ever ignored. The Napoleonic armies marched across Germany and in 1805 decisively
defeated Austria, then the principal German power; and in
the following year they destroyed with swiftness and apparent
ease Prussian power and the Prussian state itself. Slowly the
writers of the day shifted their romantic enthusiasm from the
internationalism of Novalis (who had died in 1801) to a patriotic German view of poetry, history and politics.

A clear symptom of the new nationalistic romantic world
was the collection of folk-songs, *Des Knaben Wunderhorn*,
published between 1806 and 1808 by two young men, Arnim
and Brentano. The *Wunderhorn*, which was widely read and
highly praised by many including Goethe, was, unlike Herder's *Volkslieder*, a purely German collection. The patriotism
it implied soon became more explicit, as military defeat and
oppressive occupation provoked resistance. But as so often
happens, the great political events of patriotic revival and
military liberation evoked for the most part only trivial
poetry. The essence of romanticism, with its inward moods

83

and its limitless horizons in an indefinite landscape, remained peaceful.

The finest poet of German romanticism is just such an interpreter of nature. Joseph von Eichendorff (1788–1857), brought up in the unspoiled expanses of Silesian hills and woods, spent his life as a civil servant in Berlin, but never lost his recollection of the countryside of his childhood. A Catholic, whose faith never faltered, he could survey the shifting world from a firm point of vantage and yet remain sensitive to the dark forces threatening the soul. Eichendorff does not portray an objective landscape, but catches the diverse moods of man in contact with nature. With an inexplicable magic touch (he himself speaks of the *Zauberwort*), he creates evocative, bewitchingly beautiful poetry out of the simplest and most familiar verbal material. He wrote novels as well, though these, because of diffuse presentation, have never won much acclaim. Yet *Ahnung und Gegenwart* (1815) and *Dichter und ihre Gesellen* (1834), in spite of dated romantic apparatus, catch the tone and mood of a world balanced between promise and fulfilment. His charming story *Aus dem Leben eines Taugenichts* (1826) is the classical embodiment of the romantic rejection of convention and routine.

Eichendorff studied at Heidelberg and there came under the influence of Arnim, Brentano and the *Wunderhorn*, and when later he moved to Berlin, he found that the focus of romanticism had moved there too. The Schlegel brothers with their sharp-witted wives had established themselves there; Achim von Arnim (1781–1831), who might have been a better writer if he had not lived in a romantic age, was there, too, and with him was his friend Clemens Brentano (1778–1842), unstable and brilliant, the author of sensitive poetry and of the tender and tragic love story *Geschichte vom braven Casperl und dem schönen Annerl* (1838). Also in Berlin at the time were Adalbert von Chamisso (1781–1838), a French *émigré* and Prussian officer, whose tale *Peter Schlemihls wundersame Geschichte* (1814) reflects both his own situation and the political plight of Prussia under French domination, and Friedrich de la Motte Fouqué (1777–1843), whose French origins lie farther back. Most of Fouqué's romantic writing is

84

trivial and superficial, but his story *Undine* (1811), telling of the love of a knight for a water sprite, comes alive with astonishing and eerie beauty.

This Berlin romanticism diverged steadily further from the rapt tenderness of Eichendorff's poetry, the pathos of Brentano's *Casperl* or the compelling landscape of *Undine*, becoming ever more intellectualised as it was caught up in the small (and sometimes large) talk of literary salons. The really great and independent writer of Berlin was E. T. A. Hoffmann (1776–1822), no society lion but a Prussian civil servant with eccentric habits and an addiction to drink. In a long series of stories, grouped in collections with fantastic names – *Fantasiestücke in Callots Manier* (1814), *Nachtstücke* (1817), *Die Serapionsbrüder* (1819) – Hoffmann evoked a world of convincing realism into which the supernatural and the horrifying stealthily creep. Among these masterpieces, *Der goldne Topf* (in which the conflict of reality and the uncanny is played out with exquisite poetry and outrageously grotesque humour (and *Das Fräulein von Scuderi* (in which the irrational is conceived in terms of psychopathology) are outstanding. Hoffmann also wrote a frightening but impressive novel of a schizophrenic personality (*Die Elixiere des Teufels*, 1815) and an amusing and penetrating fantasy of dual existence with *Kater Murr* (1820–2). He was also a gifted musician who wrote and composed a three-act opera *Undine* (1812) based on Fouqué's story.

The romantic movement in Germany had had its great nature poet in Eichendorff; there had been phases of overpowering emotion which rose to their greatest intensity in the death-wish of Novalis; it had sensed the sinister (*die Nachtseite* of nature and of life), had turned to the old German past and to the Christian religion of the Middle Ages. It was extraordinarily fertile, and later literature cannot be imagined without it. But as a movement it now began to fade away. Already the partial realism of Hoffmann was symptomatic of a change. In the far south-west, so often behind the times, romanticism still flourished in the writing of an eccentric doctor, Justinus Kerner (1786–1862), or in a historical novel such as *Lichtenstein* by Wilhelm Hauff (1802–27); but Ludwig Uhland (1787–1862) disposed of his romantic phase by the time he was thirty and thereafter devoted himself to political idealism instead of poetry. Only isolated stragglers, such as the mentally ill poet of despair Nikolaus Lenau (1802–50), carried pure romantic writing into the middle of the nineteenth century.

One poet stands out as the heir to romanticism and simultaneously as the herald of a new world of political as well as literary realism. Heinrich Heine (1797–1856), the first Jewish writer of real stature in German literature, began with derivative romantic poems and tragedies. In 1826 he achieved a success with a humorous, whimsical travel book, *Die Harzreise*, and in the following year he published a substantial volume of verse, *Das Buch der Lieder*, which quickly earned him a European reputation. These early poems, passionate, tender, ironic and facetious by turns, have, rather unfairly, gone out of fashion, and attention has been concentrated on Heine's middle and later verse. As Heine grew older, his poetry acquired a cutting edge and a political bias. *Deutschland. Ein Wintermärchen* (1844) and *Atta Troll* (1847) are pungent yet attractive satires directed by a brilliant intellect. Heine's greatest work is in the poems of the *Romanzero* (1851) and *Letzte Gedichte* (1853–5). Here the sense of beauty is as strong as ever, but the dreams are abandoned as he grapples courageously and astringently with a harsh reality. The self-ironisation recorded in his poems was the weapon with which he fought his way through his own slow death.

2. *Two Great Outsiders*

The greatest authors can rarely be comprehended inside the framework of a single movement. This is hardly surprising, for movements are summaries of shared characteristics and the great writers are the original exceptions. Two such distinctive figures, who are in the romantic period but only partly of it, are Kleist and Grillparzer.

In a short life, to which he put an end himself, Heinrich von Kleist (1777–1811) wrote a handful of plays and stories of highly individual character. At sixteen a Prussian officer and at nineteen an experienced campaigner, Kleist resigned his commission in 1799 and lived experimentally as a littérateur and in various brief jobs. A perfectionist who could not compromise, he destroyed *Robert Guiskard*, perhaps his finest work, and only a fragment of it remains. His own obsessive mind created characters governed by obsessions and victims of delusion. The problem of identity besets them, and though in the play *Das Käthchen von Heilbronn* (1810) and the story *Die Marquise von O.* (1808) the problem is happily resolved, in others, such as the tragedy *Penthesilea* and the stories *Das Erdbeben in Chili* (1807) and *Die Verlobung in St Domingo* (1811), it ends in heartrending catastrophe. In two works the conflicting forces of human existence are held in perfect balance, in the tragic story *Michael Kohlhaas* and in the *Schauspiel Prinz Friedrich von Homburg* (1821). Kleist is one of the greatest German writers, for his prose and his verse are alike dynamic and significant in every phrase of every sentence. Though he had no outward connection with romanticism, it is probable that the extremity of his character would have had greater difficulty in expressing itself in a more equable mental and moral climate.

The other marginal poet of this age, Franz Grillparzer (1791–1872), lived all his life in Vienna, a city which in his youth was remote from the main stream of German literary life, though it had the finest musical culture in Europe. Hypersensitive and gifted with immense understanding of the human heart, Grillparzer wrote a number of plays in which a romantic mobility of emotion is expressed in classical or historical terms. *Sappho* (1819) is a tragedy in which poetry fails to compensate for the defeat of love. In *Das goldene Vliess* (1822) the tenderest sentiments are scorched and withered by ambition. And *Des Meeres und der Liebe Wellen* (1840) treats with subtlety and sensitiveness the tragic story of Hero's love for Leander. The plays of Austrian history, *König Ottokars Glück und Ende* (1825) and *Ein treuer Diener seines Herrn* (1830), present in a patriotic setting the themes of measureless ambition and unstinting, selfless devotion which fascinated Grillparzer. But the intensely introspective poet was too easily hurt to be a successful man of the stage, and when his comedy *Weh' dem, der lügt!* failed in 1838, he withdrew from the theatre for good. Yet in spite of outward silence he wrote in his own privacy three more remarkable tragedies, of which *Ein Bruderzwist in Habsburg* (1872), dealing with Rudolph II, is perhaps his finest work.

Kleist wrote his plays in the stresses of Napoleonic conquest and occupation, of political expansion and political disintegration. In 1803 he had thought of satisfying his latent death-wish by enlisting in the army which Napoleon was then collecting at Boulogne for an invasion of England. By a characteristic swing of his extreme nature his last years were consumed by a savage hatred of Napoleon, the oppressor since 1806 of Kleist's own country, Prussia. Impatient, unsatisfied, uncompromising, he expressed more truly than most the tensions of the time. Grillparzer, half a generation younger, began to write in the peace which followed Waterloo, a time of disillusionment, of middle-class quietism, of unrest among the young, and of fear of a ubiquitous secret police. Though he stands aloof, the dignity of his personality and the sense of failure which besets so many of his characters show the response of a sensitive man to an age which strangled the illusions of a whole generation.

8 The Mid-Century: 1830–1880

1. The Search for New Forms: 1830–1850

The quiet years between Waterloo and the international revolution of 1848 are sometimes seen as the age of *Biedermeier*, a term suggesting middle-class restraint, parochial vision, respect for the aristocracy and gentry, and altogether an enclosed, modest world of limited horizons, limited fortunes and limited virtues. Perhaps the word ought to be reserved for a style of furniture, solid and well-proportioned, and for a robust, neat and comfortable architecture – Regency without the elegance. As a literary term it is questionable. Writers may have *Biedermeier* facets, but no author of merit conforms fully to the theoretical pattern. This sober society under the shadow of the repression of the Metternich system suffered a shock when the stability of the new world, masquerading as the old pre-Revolutionary world, was suddenly shaken by the Paris Revolution of 1830, and the definitive flight of the Bourbon monarchs. Though Germany showed no more than sympathetic unrest, the new revolution marked all the same a stage in German history. 1830 gave notice to all Europe that revolution was not extinct, only dormant – and that it could erupt again. It effectively drew a line beneath the romantic movement which, dreaming its dreams, had left the real world alone.

The writers of the next generation began a search for new means of expression. Two possibilities faced them. They could hold the old course and go beyond existing romanticism into a world of violent, cruel and horrifying fantasy; or they could abandon dreams and portray the real world as it is. Grabbe chose the first course, Büchner the second. Christian Dietrich Grabbe (1801–36) was never able to come to terms with his environment, with his family or even with himself. His plays seem to be futile gestures of self-assertion, piling horror upon horror, until horror overreaches itself and boredom supervenes. But Grabbe had a real talent, visible in occasional poetic flashes and once realised in full in an astonishing 'epic' play which presents in realistic snatches the figure of the doomed Napoleon (*Napoleon oder die hundert Tage*, 1831). Georg Büchner (1813–37), a revolutionary student on the run, achieved a moving poetic effect in his realistic historical tragedy *Dantons Tod* (1835), and in the remarkable unfinished play *Woyzeck* he created the expressionistic tragedy of the common man eighty years before its time.

Ferdinand Freiligrath (1810–76) and Georg Herwegh (1817–75) both wrote political poetry in the forties which gained a much greater following than Grabbe and Büchner enjoyed, but their work now seems to attitudinise with the gestures of a romantic age which was already dead. Karl Gutzkow (1811–78), the most notable of the Liberal group of writers called *Jung-Deutschland*, had a more versatile talent; but lacking depth and originality, he produced estimable works which are now no longer read except for motives of duty. His novel *Wally die Zweiflerin* (1835), once intended to shock, has lost its power to do so, and his earnest and well-intentioned plays (e.g. *Uriel Acosta*, 1847) seem devitalised. Yet his enormous conspectus of contemporary life, the novel *Die Ritter vom Geiste* (1850 f.) is a near-masterpiece which has suffered undeserved neglect.

Beside all this political commotion Karl Immermann (1796–1840), though he gave Grabbe encouragement and helped some of his plays on to the stage, deliberately exploited romantic forms, knowing them to be outworn and accepting with irony his role as a belated straggler. He is the author of two eccentric novels, *Die Epigonen* (1836), which stands between a great age which is spent and a future which is distasteful, and *Münchhausen* (1838), a faded satire which contains an inserted village story of great power and savour. It has been published separately as *Der Oberhof* and is a landmark in the growth of a new type of narrative, the *Dorfgeschichte*.

Just as Immermann died, a new and original writer made

his public appearance. Friedrich Hebbel (1813–63), touchy, sensitive, self-taught and iron-willed, began with a biblical tragedy, *Judith* (1840), in which two powerful wills collide at a moment of historic crisis. Hebbel went his own individual way, linking up in *Maria Magdalena* (1844) with the *bürgerliches Trauerspiel*, and in other plays with the tradition of poetic historical drama; but always his plays express individual thought and their technique is a closely wrought texture in which no word is lost. In *Genoveva* (1843), *Gyges und sein Ring* (1856) and *Die Nibelungen* (1862) he used legends to portray the timeless essentials of man; and in *Herodes und Mariamne* (1850) and especially in the prose *Agnes Bernauer* (1855) he draws on history to reflect in equally valid terms the human situation in its duality of society and individual. Neglected in recent years, he is due for a revival.

Hebbel was an idiosyncratic thinker, yet some of his thought, particularly his theory that the course of human history follows from action and reaction, combining to produce a synthesis, which in turn provokes a new reaction, so that the process continues *ad infinitum*, has a close resemblance to an aspect of Hegel's philosophy. Friedrich Hegel (1770–1831), a professor of philosophy at various universities, set out from the basis of Kant's idealism and treated religious, political, historical and artistic phenomena as expressions of a spirit (*Geist*) becoming more and more articulate. Hegel's influence on German learning and thought was immense and still continues, but the creative writers have remained largely immune. The philosophy of Arthur Schopenhauer (1788–1860), on the other hand, had a special appeal for artists and poets, and the grandiose pessimism of his outlook swayed artists as diverse as Richard Wagner and Thomas Mann.

2. Poetic Realism: 1850–1870

The Revolution of 1848 disrupted Germany and shook the even tenor of the citizen's life, giving warning for the third time (after 1789 and 1830) that violent change was becoming endemic in Europe. But experience shows over and over again that literature does not necessarily reflect such apparent historical truths. The reason is that the reality of an age, as felt by its own contemporaries, may be very different from our later historical generalisation. After 1848 there is no great stream of revolutionary literature, nor any barrier of works opposing revolution. In the lives of the citizens the wounds soon healed, commerce and social life resumed their courses, and a literature of the private individual prevailed. It was primarily a literature about the citizen middle class (*Bürgertum*), written for that middle class. The burgher had become the bearer of civilised and cultural values in the eighteenth century. In the nineteenth he consolidated his position. The crowds of poor workers, outcome of the drift to the towns, had not yet coalesced into a class. The rural population, necessarily scattered, could not become articulate. The aristocracy, small in numbers, was losing its own standards and drifting towards the burgher's point of view. But the strength of the burgher's position became his weakness. Self-complacency and a rigid pattern of behaviour, termed respectability, asserted themselves. In this restrictive mental climate many writers felt it to be their task to champion an idealism that the citizen class would respect and so to establish civilised values which were threatened by materialism and indifference.

To this considerable body of writing, largely composed of novels and *Novellen*, the term 'poetic realism' is often applied. This phrase, adopted by Otto Ludwig,[1] implies a realism tempered by selection, the truth, so to speak, but not the whole truth. It is only fair to point out that the writers themselves saw the truth residing in the immanent idealism, rather than in the detailed portrayal of life. The roots of poetic realism are in the romantic movement, and a poet whose earliest work, *Maler Nolten* (1832), was a romantic novel about an artist, foreshadows the new view of literature. Eduard Mörike (1804–75), whose first collected volume of poems appeared in 1838, was a Württemberg pastor who never felt at home with his pastoral duties and eventually went on permanent sick leave. Though an indifferent clergyman, he was one of the most sensitive and subtle German poets. It is sometimes said that

[1] See below, p. 95.

his range is narrow, yet it extends from heart-breaking tragedy to ironical comedy; and he has an equal command of folk-song stanzas, sonnets and classical measures. His verse has a delicate precision which responds to every nuance of feeling. And one side of his poetry, poems capturing brief episodes of contemporary life such as 'Abreise', or longer whimsical reflections of character like 'Der alte Turmhahn' suggests the new realistic trend of the fifties and sixties.

Roughly contemporary with Mörike was the Westphalian poetess Annette von Droste-Hülshoff (1797–1848). Brought up in the restrictive conditions imposed on a woman of good family in the early nineteenth century, she was forty-one before she was able to publish her first volume, *Gedichte*, which coincided with Mörike's *Gedichte* in 1838. Her verse, which is largely nature poetry, directs a new vision to its subject, disregarding landscape conventions and penetrating to the reality of colour, shape and movement. Droste is also the author of a *Novelle*, her only work of fiction, which initiates the manner of poetic realism in story-telling and is not surpassed by any later example. *Die Judenbuche* (1842) is a vivid evocation of the Westphalian countryside and peasantry of the preceding century and simultaneously a reticent and moving tragedy.

Droste wrote of the country because it was her own environment, but it is noticeable that practically all the literature grouped as poetic realism has a rural or small-town setting, whatever the background of the author. It is perhaps a legacy of the romantic outlook from Rousseau to Eichendorff, and, moveover, in that age of incipient industrialism the country could be regarded as the idealistic stronghold of poetry in face of the new urban squalor. Berthold Auerbach[1] (1812–82), a Jew who spent most of his life in large towns and was active in politics as a Liberal, wrote a succession of stories set in the Black Forest environment of his childhood (*Schwarzwälder Dorfgeschichten*, 1843–4), which express the townsman's yearning for the simplicity and freshness of the country. Auerbach's village stories seem now to have an urban refinement, but to the city readers of the mid-century they brought a breath of pure country air. His neglected novels (*Auf der*

[1] This was a pseudonym. His real name was Moyses Baruch.

Höhe, 1865, *Das Landhaus am Rhein*, 1869) discuss acutely the social tensions of the age.

A much greater novelist had been writing in Switzerland before Auerbach began to publish, but his reputation remained for a long time merely local. Jeremias Gotthelf was the pseudonym of Albert Bitzius (1797–1854), a country parson who wrote for his own farming and labouring parishioners and those of the other Swiss valleys. He began with impressive pictures of the dark side of Swiss rural life (*Der Bauernspiegel*, 1837, *Leiden und Freuden eines Schulmeisters*, 1838) and then produced a succession of novels of the countryside in which the satirical bias is less pronounced and a balance is held between the admirable qualities and the evils and abuses of Swiss life. The most famous of these novels is *Wie Uli der Knecht glücklich wird* (1841), the story of a young labourer's struggle with himself, but *Wie Anne Bäbi Jowäger haushaltet* (1843) and *Geld und Geist* (1844) are finer still. Gotthelf, who was equally at home in the more compressed and demanding form of the *Novelle* (*Elsi die seltsame Magd*, *Hans Joggeli der Erbvetter* and *Die schwarze Spinne*), had the plainest of didactic intentions, but he had also the power and resource to create varied character and a gift for lucid, forceful and racy expression.

Each of these writers reflects a particular locality, Droste her Westphalian homeland, Gotthelf the Swiss parishes of the Berne district, and Auerbach the Black Forest valley in which he spent his childhood. The extreme form of this regionalism is found in dialect literature, which continued the tradition of J. P. Hebel,[1] adding a new self-conscious, almost conservationist, note. The two great dialect writers of the age (both speaking Low German) appeared at almost the same moment, the Holsteiner Klaus Groth (1819–99) with the tender lyric poetry of *Quickborn* (1852) and the Mecklenburger Fritz Reuter (1810–74) with his humorous verse tales *Läuschen un Rimels* (1853), followed by a series of partly autobiographical novels, *Ut de Franzosentid* (1859), *Ut mine Festungstid* (1862) and *Ut mine Stromtid* (1862–64), which are full of rich, humorous character portrayal.

[1] (1760–1826)

94

The least obviously regional novelist of this time was Adalbert Stifter (1805–68), of Austrian nationality, a German-speaker from the Bohemian Forest district of what since 1918 has been Czecho-Slovakia. Stifter was a man of high idealistic purpose, and the local element in his work is screened by the discipline and restraint of his style. His whole oeuvre is built upon gradualness, on a sense of gentle development, imperceptible growth and timely fruition. His stories (*Der Hochwald*, 1842, *Brigitta*, 1843, and the collection *Bunte Steine*, 1853) and his novel *Der Nachsommer* (1857) were slow to win readers because they lacked anything sensational, and it is only in the twentieth century that the rounded wholeness of his novels has come to be appreciated. Far from being facile or lax, their serenity arises from a finely poised and precariously held balance.

The Thuringian Otto Ludwig (1813–65) wanted above all to shine in drama, which he rated as the highest form of literature. Yet, though he had one popular success in the atmospheric forest play *Der Erbförster* (1853), he lost his way in endless ponderings on dramatic theory; and his reputation now rests, ironically enough, on two works of fiction which he valued less. *Die Heiteretei* (1854) is a narrative comedy in which the mock-heroic and the movingly human are humorously intertwined. This adventure into the village story is surpassed by *Zwischen Himmel und Erde* (1856), a powerful novel or *Novelle* (it seems a compromise between the two), in which dark passions and inhibiting virtues clash before a background of the steeplejack's and slater's life in a small-town environment.

Probably more young people have made their first acquaintance with German literature through *Immensee* (1851) than through any other work. It is short, clear, has a pervasive sadness and wistful fragrance and is supported by an easily understood symbolism. If Theodor Storm (1817–88), its author, was a poetic realist, he also gave a hint of the evocative, atmospheric art to which the name 'impressionism' is often given. Almost the whole of Storm's work is small in scale. Its background is the German borderland of Schleswig-Holstein, its problems are personal and its form is the *Novelle* and especially the short *Novelle*. Only towards the end of his life, with more ambitious stories such as *Aquis submersus* (1877), *Renate* (1878) and notably the tragic story *Der Schimmelreiter* (1888), did he attempt something more weighty; yet even these, by the buffering effect of their 'framed presentation' – a story within a story – remain modest in proportion and scope.

Two writers of this central phase of the century attempted something outside the personal affairs of the individual. Gottfried Keller (1819–90), a Swiss, tried to make a career as a painter, failed and turned instead to letters, beginning with an autobiographical novel, *Der grüne Heinrich* (1854). His later work consists chiefly of *Novellen*, grouped in collections; of these *Die Leute von Seldwyla* (1856), which contains the village tragedy *Romeo und Julia auf dem Dorfe*, and *Das Sinngedicht* (1882), which synthesises a set of stories into a single work, are the best known. Underlying Keller's work is a sincere but somewhat joyless social devotion; his individuals are framed in a society which demands from them more than it gives.

Gustav Freytag (1816–95), the other social writer, was an academic turned journalist and author, and was the most characteristic and articulate representative of the middle class which in the decade of German unification (1862–71) provided Bismarck with much of his support. Freytag's outstanding work is the business novel *Soll und Haben* (1855), which embodies the vigour and thrustfulness, the tenacity and integrity of the commercial middle class of that generation. It is an apotheosis of *Tüchtigkeit*, with its implications of honest industry and limited vision. Freytag turned later to historical writing in a nationalistic sense, and though his personality is not aggressive, it is clear that his writing has a certain insensitive robustness, which won it readers at the time and has lost it its reputation since.

3. The New Germany

The old fragmented Germany survived well into the nineteenth century. But the railways and factories which transformed the landscape and changed the lives of so many people were not compatible with the easy-going world of the eighteenth century. Prussia, the one really efficient German state, took over the lead and created a new Germany in its own image. The sixties, in which such poetic or idealistic works as Storm's *Auf der Universität*, Raabe's *Der Hungerpastor*, Freytag's *Die verlorene Handschrift* or Stifter's *Witiko* were published, were also the years of the short, sharp wars (1864, 1866 and 1870) by which Prussia asserted its ascendency and assimilated its companions.

The emergence of a new Empire was accompanied by an upsurge of prosperity and a wave of materialism. A self-conscious cult of 'Germanness' spread even to the Church and the universities. The new climate of self-confident assertion seemed incapable of fostering a living art and literature. This was the heyday of the *Professorenroman*, the historical novel with accurate archaeological detail but a devitalised nineteenth-century spirit, such as *Der Kampf um Rom* (1876) by Felix Dahn (1834–1912) and *Uarda* (1877) by Georg Ebers (1837–98). And even the success of the music dramas (*Musikdramen*) of Richard Wagner (1813–83) was due, not so much to their unaccustomed musical idiom, to their perceptive psychology and symbolic mythology, as to the Germanic origins of their stories.

Here and there the old traditions held firm or a promise appeared of something new. Friedrich Spielhagen (1829–1911), an almost forgotten name, maintained the Liberal line of the mid-century right into the new era with a series of acute and arresting, but sometimes pretentious, novels such as *Problematische Naturen* (1861), *In Reih' und Glied* (1866) and *Hammer und Amboss* (1868–9), reflecting the decline of the aristocracy and the rise of the middle class. Less popular at the time but endowed with far greater creative power was Wilhelm Raabe (1831–1910), who began with Dickensian novels such as *Die Chronik der Sperlingsgasse* (1857) and *Der Hungerpastor* (1864) and went on to produce a number of compact and close-wrought stories, reflecting with humour and irony the short-lived joys and manifold tribulations of life and simultaneously affirming tolerance and compassion as the

D

human qualities which enable sensitive men to live in a harsh and unjust world. Among these short novels *Das Odfeld* (1889), *Stopfkuchen* (1891) and *Hastenbeck* (1898) are outstanding; they assert independence and deep feeling in an age which opted for sedative cliché or ostentatious declamation.

Independent in a different way was Conrad Ferdinand Meyer (1825–98), after Gotthelf and Keller the third great Swiss writer of the century. A 'late developer', Meyer was long hesitant and uncertain of himself. His earliest ballad poetry appeared in 1864, his first story (*Das Amulett*) in 1873 and his collected poems in 1882. Meyer did not like the world he lived in and his *Novellen* are a flight into the past. Yet to label them as 'escapist' is to pass too facile a judgement. His carefully fashioned stories, mostly of medieval or renaissance life, are balanced and fastidious commentaries on human affairs, even though they make no allusion to contemporary conditions. Of many titles which deserve mention, *Der Schuss von der Kanzel* (1877), *Der Heilige* (1879), which deals with Thomas à Becket, and *Gustav Adolfs Page* (1882) are among the best. Meyer's cool, finely wrought poems display a reticent symbolism which in some degree anticipates Rilke's 'object poems' (*Dinggedichte*).

In contrast to the Swiss burgher who turned from the present to aristocratic environments in the past, Marie von Ebner-Eschenbach (1830–1916), an Austrian noblewoman from Moravia, whose social life moved in the accepted patterns of her class, wrote novels and stories of convincing realism animated by an understanding sympathy for the humble and the poor. With *Das Gemeindekind* (1887) and *Dorf– und Schlossgeschichten* (1883) she comes near to converting realism into naturalism, but her writing has not power enough to give her books continued currency after eighty years.

Apart from the complex and highly organised mythical music dramas of Richard Wagner (1813–83), which reached their summit of recognition in the first performance of *Der Ring des Nibelungen* at the Bayreuth *Festspiele* in 1876, dramatic writing was at a low ebb in the sixties and seventies. Hebbel and Otto Ludwig were dead, Grillparzer kept silent.

The public went to the theatre to be amused and the principal fare consisted of vacuous comedies and farces, many of which were imported from France. The only new German dramatist of note between 1850 and 1880 was the Austrian Ludwig Anzengruber (1839–89), who with local plays such as *Das vierte Gebot* (1878), a dialect tragedy, continued a Viennese tradition of unliterary, popular plays which had earlier been represented by Ferdinand Raimund (1790–1836) and Johann Nepomuk Nestroy (1801–62). Anzengruber broke new ground with rural popular plays (*Volksstücke*) such as *Der Pfarrer von Kirchfeld* (1871) and *Die Kreuzelschreiber* (1872). The serious presentation of the rural poor and the city proletariat in these plays was a step towards a new realism, and so too was the consistent use of dialect. Nevertheless Anzengruber's plays, with their conventional action and inserted songs, remained primarily a Viennese entertainment.

Towards the end of the century three writers of an older generation, Fontane, Liliencron and Spitteler, brought a new and vigorous life into literature. Theodor Fontane (1819–98), a Prussian of French extraction, for many years wrote competent ballads and attractive accounts of Prussian topography and history. Then, at the age of sixty, he took to novel-writing and in his last twenty years wrote sixteen novels. The best of these form a group of eight stories of contemporary Berlin society, of which the highlights are *Irrungen Wirrungen* (1888), *Frau Jenny Treibel* (1892) and *Effi Briest* (1895). In these Fontane combines thorough local knowledge, accurate observation, a brilliant sense for dialogue, a perception of social forces and a warm human sympathy. His technique of using observed detail to reveal the reality below the surface was mistaken by many for a naturalistic devotion to minutiae, winning him the favour of a new generation with which his independent temperament was not in sympathy.

Detlev von Liliencron (1844–1909), an officer with a real talent and taste for soldiering, found himself obliged, because of debt, to leave the service. In after years he managed to incorporate some of his war experiences in poetry of striking vigour and originality (*Adjutantenritte*, 1883). A very uneven poet, he is capable of terse and powerful statement and sentimental banality in one and the same poem. At his best he has an inventive energy in the handling of words which is almost unique.

The third of these remarkable individuals in a conformist age was Carl Spitteler (1845–1924). Spitteler, who was a Swiss, set out in one sense to put the clock back, for in *Olympischer Frühling* (1900–6) he revived the obsolescent verse epic; yet his psychological and philosophical standpoint is unflinchingly modern. Since repeated attempts to gain a hearing for his epics have made no headway, they must by now be reckoned splendid failures. His novel *Imago* (1906) has also had no more than a *succès d'estime*, and yet it exploits convincingly the modern methods of psychological analysis associated with Freud.

The most remarkable mind of all the individualists writing in the years 1870–90 was Friedrich Nietzsche (1844–1900), who became a university professor at twenty-six and went out of his mind nineteen years later. Nietzsche has often been held responsible for the aggressiveness of German nationalism and for National Socialism which ultimately grew out of it. And it is true that certain myths created by him (notably the superman – *der Übermensch*) and his contrasting concepts of *Herrenmoral* and *Sklavenmoral* were easily adapted to base ends and used to justify ruthless expediency, exploitation and cruelty. Yet Nietzsche's work is not in itself arrogantly aggressive. His sensitive, searching mind examined nineteenth-century civilisation, questioning its conventional values and stripping it of its pretences. The bitterness of his tone in such searing criticisms as *Menschliches Allzumenschliches* (1878) or *Jenseits von Gut und Böse* (1886) arises from a sense of powerlessness. The positive side of his writings, of which the hectic dithyrambic *Also sprach Zarathustra* (1883–91) is the climax, was less successful and more dangerous. But whatever Nietzsche touched he illuminated, and in one of his earliest works, *Die Geburt der Tragödie aus dem Geiste der Musik* (1873), he revolutionised the accepted view of Greek art, setting the dynamic tragic Dionysiac principle beside the Apolline serenity which Winckelmann had emphasised. Though by playing the prophet Nietzsche eased the sense of an unfulfilled mission, his greatness lies in his penetrating and fearless criticism. He was one of the great social diagnosticians and his doctrine, however much it was later misused, had nothing to do with the materialistic nationalism on which the German Empire of 1871 was built.

9 The Literature of Our Age

1. New Paths are Found: 1885–1914

It was in the nature of individualists like Raabe and Fontane to be concerned with their own particular art and to be disinclined to preach a doctrine or establish a school. And Nietzsche, who certainly had a message, and spoke it with ruthless emphasis, so strongly disliked the mass that he virtually discouraged all co-operation. The more radical minds were nevertheless deeply dissatisfied with the society which had developed in the new industrial and Imperial Germany. They resented not only the wealth of the rich and the poverty of the new proletariat, they were also hostile to the conscious division of mental life into two entirely separate compartments, on the one hand the rasping, aggressive, opportunist life of every day, and on the other a serene and detached world of art and poetry and music which could afford agreeable relaxation from the more serious and important business of money-making.

The first real thrust on a broad front towards a new literature was an attempt to abolish the severance between art and life. The means lay to hand. Realistic techniques of description and presentation had been evolved by Annette von Droste-Hülshoff, Otto Ludwig and even Theodor Storm, and abroad they had been developed much more extensively and thoroughly by Zola and Tolstoy, who invested the novel with a stark, disturbing realism, and by Ibsen, then living in Germany, who applied a similar technique to the drama and the theatre, creating in the 1880s a succession of plays which could be read as a searing criticism of contemporary society.

In this new stirring of social conscience and literary originality Germany was perhaps a decade behind its eastern, western and northern neighbours. Although minor writers and publicists such as the brothers Hart and Wilhelm Bölsche served as straws in the wind in the preceding years, the real impact came in 1889. In that year Gerhart Hauptmann's first play, *Vor Sonnenaufgang*, was performed at the theatre club called *Die Freie Bühne*, and the stories grouped as *Papa Hamlet* were published by the co-authors Arno Holz and Johannes Schlaf under a Norwegian pseudonym, Bjarne P. Holmsen. In 1890 a play by Holz and Schlaf, *Die Familie Selicke*, was produced; so too was a second play by Hauptmann (*Das Friedensfest*) and one by Sudermann (*Die Ehre*). These plays became the focus of violent opposition and equally violent partisanship, and they were the forerunners of a spate of works which dealt with social and moral problems with intransigent seriousness and supposedly exact and lifelike detail. They were especially concerned to drag into the open matters which society wished to disregard; they directed themselves at two principal points of unjust exploitation, the industrial poor and the underprivileged woman.

Arno Holz (1853–1929) and Johannes Schlaf (1862–1941), who had co-operated for a brief spell, soon fell out, and Schlaf, after writing on his own the tragedy *Meister Oelze* (1892), ceased to be of importance to the new movement. Holz by his fertility of mind and restless intelligence became the most influential theorist of naturalism, as the new movement came to be called. *Die Kunst, ihr Wesen und ihre Gesetze*, in which he coined for the new style of writing the term *konsequenter Naturalismus*, was its manifesto. In his stories Holz developed a detailed exploitation of reality, a so-called *Sekundenstil*, which encouraged original observation of *minutiae*, but tended inevitably to drag out seconds into much longer intervals of time. As the impulse which Holz had given to naturalism flagged, he turned to the cultivation of more imaginative uses of language in *Phantasus* (1898) and *Dafnis* (1904).

The tragedy *Vor Sonnenaufgang* thrust Gerhart Hauptmann (1862–1946), hitherto unknown, into the fiercest light of public controversy. Its presentation of alcoholism, industrial exploitation and obstinate idealism touched sore points of social conscience, and its brilliant realism, in which Silesian dialect figures prominently, gave it a form as new and topical as its content. This play loosed off in Hauptmann a spell of extraordinary dramatic fertility. For the next five years he wrote at least one play a year, all of them naturalistic. The serious plays *Das Friedensfest* and *Einsame Menschen* appeared respectively in 1890 and 1891, followed by two comedies, one of which, *Der Biberpelz* (1893) a good-humoured and witty satire of resourceful dishonesty versus stupid officialdom, is sometimes reckoned his best work. *Die Weber* (1892), a semi-historical play about the weavers' riots of 1844, makes an original and powerful, though ultimately unsuccessful, attempt to substitute the mass for the individual as a hero of tragedy. *Hanneles Himmelfahrt* (1894) aroused a doubt of Hauptmann's devotion to naturalism, a doubt which was confirmed by the poetic parable play of his own emotional and artistic life, *Die versunkene Glocke* (1897). From then on he was repeatedly attracted to poetic and symbolic plays such as *Der arme Heinrich* (1902), *Und Pippa tanzt* (1906), *Festspiel in deutschen Reimen* (1913) and *Atridentetralogie* (1941–8). And he was equally often drawn back to naturalism with *Fuhrmann Henschel* (1899), *Rose Bernd* (1903) and *Die Ratten* (1911). All three are splendidly written plays and deeply moving records of human suffering. A capacity for creating character and a gift for apt and fluent dialogue commend Hauptmann's plays, just as a flickering uncertainty of purpose often blurs their effect. Hauptmann wrote a few novels, of which *Der Narr in Christo Emanuel Quint* (1910) can be read as a study of delusive religious obsession or as a spiritual parable; *Das Buch der Leidenschaft* (1929) is an erotic autobiography in fictional disguise. His outstanding *Novelle* is *Bahnwärter Thiel* (1892), a remarkable and paradoxical fusion of the naturalistic and the poetic. This tragic story of the meek railway crossing keeper and his gross second wife, in a setting in which forest and railway harmonise, demonstrated the emotional overtones which could be derived from the new technical elements of society.

In *Die Ehre* (1890), a satirical commentary on the conventional code of honour, and even more in *Heimat* (1893), with its conflict of Bohemianism and respectability in a family reunion, Hermann Sudermann (1857–1928) was even more successful in drawing large audiences than Hauptmann. But it soon became clear that, as a dramatist, he was no more than a competent commercial writer with a flair for the fashion of the moment. These are not negligible qualities, but they are not those of the true pioneers and geniuses. His best work for the theatre is the one-act tragedy *Fritzchen* (1896). Though they were overshadowed by his dramatic work, the novels *Frau Sorge* (1887) and *Der Katzensteg* (1889) are not without distinction, and the late group of stories published as *Litauische Geschichten* (1917) is perhaps his highest achievement.

Max Kretzer (1854–1951), a factory worker and a convinced Social Democrat, sought to apply naturalist technique to the novel, beginning with *Die beiden Genossen* (1880). His outstanding novel is *Meister Timpe* (1888), which deals with the submergence of the individual craftsman beneath the flood of mass production. Though Kretzer possessed depth of social feeling and passionate sincerity, he lacked both the creative imagination and the technique to make these qualities fully effective in his work. Other writers trailed in the wake of the naturalistic pioneers, among them Ernst von Wildenbruch (1845–1909), who switched from successful historical drama (*Die Quitzows*, 1888) to the naturalistic *Die Haubenlerche* (1891), and Otto Erich Hartleben (1854–1905), whose military tragedy *Rosenmontag* (1900) achieved an immense success on the stage. Others adopted much of the naturalists' technique and employed it in new ways. Arthur Schnitzler (1862–1931), who began with completely naturalistic plays, soon developed in the cycle of one-act plays entitled *Anatol* (1894) a style in which detailed realism is used to evoke an atmosphere which can rightly be called poetic. His most celebrated play is the tragedy *Liebelei* (1895), a love story in which sweetness and tenderness turn to bitter suffering. *Reigen*, a cycle of ten erotic dialogues, in each of which there is a change of partners (published 1903, performed 1920), achieved in later years considerable success as the film *La Ronde*. His satirical comedy *Professor Bernhardi* (1912) is a brilliant and provocative treatment of the problem of anti-Semitism with an intentionally indecisive end. Though Schnitzler first made his name with plays, he was also a prolific writer of prose fiction, especially *Novellen*, and it is here that his best work is found. His speciality is the penetrating and ruthless analysis of human motive, in which he demonstrates his conviction, shared by Sigmund Freud in his psychology of the subconscious, that an erotic egoism is the principal spring of action. From the early, almost clinical story *Sterben* (1895) to the spare purposefulness and discreet symbolism of *Die Toten schweigen* (1897) Schnitzler develops, with the subtlest variations, his theme of selfishness in love. In his later years he turned his spotlight on the problems of age, still seen from an erotic angle (*Frau Beate und ihr Sohn*, 1913; *Doktor Gräsler, Badearzt*, 1917; *Casanovas Heimfahrt*, 1918), and these, together with the tragedy *Das weite Land* (1910), bear closely on his own problems, for much of his work is disguised autobiography. Occasionally Schnitzler was able to escape from the sultry world of the libido and to write a serene satire such as the interior monologue *Leutnant Gustl* (1901) or the full-length social novel *Der Weg ins Freie* (1908), a highly successful evocation of a section of effete Viennese society in the pre-1914 years.

Though naturalism is the most prominent style in the novel as well as in the drama in these years, the renewal of German literature also assumed other and more imaginative forms. Hugo von Hofmannsthal (1874–1919), a cultivated man of Jewish descent and aristocratic distinction, expressed in poetry and in prose and verse drama a clear-sighted awareness of a declining civilisation. Whether in the neurotic violence of *Elektra* (1904), in the refined indolence of the comedy *Der Schwierige* (1921) or in the tortuous symbolical play *Der Turm* (1925, revised 1927), he contemplates without self-pity and without flinching the sunset of his world. A man of great musical sensitivity, he collaborated with Richard Strauss, from the opera version of *Elektra* (1909) until his death. The best known of the six resulting operas is *Der Rosenkavalier* (1911). For a time Hofmannsthal was a disciple of Stefan George (1868–1933), though in the long run he found the master's imperious authority intolerable. George, a stylised aesthete, represented a world apparently remote from naturalism, a world of formal beauty, expressed in exalted yet severely disciplined verse, purified of the dross of everyday speech. Yet George's poetry had this in common with naturalism, that it asserted standards of austerity and stood for truth (as he saw it) against the flabbiness of the late nineteenth century. At irregular intervals he published his *Blätter für die Kunst* (1892–1919), to which his disciples contributed. After *Das Jahr der Seele* (1897) a sense of mission becomes perceptible in George's poetry; he began to feel himself the agent of a transformation and elevation of the German people, and a new tone of responsibility and urgency grows in the later collections *Der Teppich des Lebens* (1899), *Der siebente Ring* (1907), the prophetic *Der Stern des Bundes* (1914) and the visionary *Das neue Reich* (1928). George carried his fastidious insistence on aesthetic standards to the point of designing his own type and devising his own notation of punctuation, prescribing also choice paper and elegant binding. Such luxuries were of course only possible for a man of great private wealth.

George's younger contemporary, Rainer Maria Rilke (1875–1926), was a greater poet. With no financial advantages of his own he lived his own life according to his own lights, always supported by well-to-do men and women who were fascinated by his personality and spell-bound by his genius. After derivative beginnings he made a journey to Russia, an experience which led to a volume of non-Christian esoteric religious verse, *Das Stunden-Buch* (1905 – the title alludes to a medieval 'book of hours'). *Das Buch der Bilder* (1902) and still more the *Neue Gedichte* (1907–8) represent for many people the characteristic poetry of Rilke. They contain many poems (so-called *Dinggedichte*) in which Rilke seems to absorb his personality into visual objects, creating by his mastery of words a new compound of the poet and what he contemplates. Several of these poems are concerned with *objets d'art*, but the volumes also include the well-known anthology pieces 'Ritter', 'Der Panther', 'Die Flamingos' and 'Das Karussell'. The summit of Rilke's achievement is to be found in the *Sonette an Orpheus* and the *Duineser Elegien*, both published in 1923. The fifty-five sonnets, though threnodic in form, are consolatory in tone. The ten elegies range from utter despair to intense jubilation. In each of these works Rilke developed a style special to its purpose, in which words, freed from the restraints of normal syntax, describe arresting and original patterns. The Austrian poet Georg Trakl (1887–1914), whose poetry is filled with foreboding and who was shattered by the experience of war and its suffering as he saw it in Galicia, was gifted with a similar power to liberate words so that they clarify experience. In the war-poem 'Grodek', written just before his death, the barely coherent acquires a heart-rending beauty.

The rebirth of drama and the renewal of poetry notwithstanding, it was the novel that in the twentieth century became the principal artistic means of commenting on human affairs. Its first great exponent in the new generation (and for some still its greatest) was Thomas Mann (1875–1955), who portrays the *comédie humaine* with pervasive irony. His first novel, *Buddenbrooks* (1901), depicts with what at first seems naturalistic truthfulness the decline of a prosperous burgher family through three generations. Cool detachment, masterly disposition and ironic playfulness, however, gradually become evident, and these qualities grow stronger in Mann's subsequent works. In different aspects the *Novellen Tristan* (1903), *Tonio Kröger* (1903) and *Der Tod in Venedig* (1913) probe and analyse with economy and irony the equivocal position of the artist in society, a problem in which Mann felt himself deeply implicated. The last of these stories was to provide the libretto for Benjamin Britten's opera *Death in Venice* (1973). On the 'magic mountain' of Mann's long novel *Der Zauberberg* (1924, based on a stay at Davos) is lodged a sanatorium which contains a microcosm of modern civilisation, the problems and prospects of which are exposed in wide-ranging and highly intelligent discussion. The tetralogy of novels *Joseph und seine Brüder* (1933–42), the first of Mann's works to be written in exile from Nazi Germany, uses the biblical figures to set forth with great variety and endless perception and irony the perplexing dual nature of man. *Doktor Faustus* (1947), a novel revealing great musical insight, reverts to the problem of the artist in tragic terms, and Thomas Mann's last (and unfinished) major work, the novel *Bekenntnisse des Hochstaplers Felix Krull*, illuminates an analogous theme in terms of satirical comedy.

It is characteristic of Mann's work that he uses irony reticently to achieve a balance. His elder brother Heinrich (1871–1950) adopted a more strident tone in which irony is stretched to savage satire. The novel *Professor Unrat oder Das Ende eines Tyrannen* (1905, known in its film form with Marlene Dietrich as *Der blaue Engel*, 1930) is a bitter exposure of a corrupt bully of a Prussian schoolmaster. In the searing sarcasm of *Der Untertan* (1918) and of the two less successful novels *Die Armen* (1917) and *Der Kopf* (1925), grouped with it to form the so-called *Kaiserreich-Trilogie*, he pillories the sycophancy and corruption of the German Empire of William II. *Die traurige Geschichte von Friedrich dem Grossen*, published posthumously in 1960, shows the bitterness and resentment unappeased to the end. Nevertheless Heinrich Mann, who felt much more at home in France and Italy than in Germany, wrote during exile a double novel of great serenity and nobility: *Die Jugend des Königs Henri Quatre* (1935) and *Die Vollendung des Königs Henri Quatre* (1938).

An equally able satirist, the Viennese Karl Kraus (1874–1936), applied his wit and venom with ferocity in order to shatter complacency and to destroy illusions. In *Die Fackel* (1899–1936), a one-man periodical, he waged a tireless and vitriolic campaign against the Austrian Establishment, postulating precision and conscientiousness in the use of a language as a criterion of morality. *Die letzten Tage der Menschheit* (1922), Kraus' response to the lies, the corruption and the inhumanity of the 1914–18 War, takes the form of a gigantic, Faustian, Expressionist tragedy.

A satirist of another kind was the actor and cabaret artist Frank Wedekind (1863–1918), who treated the sexual problems of adolescence with tenderness as well as with irony in *Frühlings Erwachen* (1891) and, in his 'Lulu plays' (*Erdgeist*, 1895, and *Die Büchse der Pandora*, 1904), exposes the species *homo sapiens* (so-called) at its most bestial, attaining in so doing an unexpected compassion. The 'Lulu plays' are the basis of Alban Berg's unfinished opera *Lulu* (1937). The emptiness and snobbery of pre-1914 middle-class society was skilfully and amusingly satirised by C. Sternheim (1878–1942) in a series of comedies grouped as *Aus dem bürgerlichen Hel-*

denleben, of which the most notable are *Die Hose* (1911), *Bürger Schippel* (1913) and *Der Snob* (1914).

The thirty years before the First World War saw a shift in the political pattern of Germany. The monarchy was still absolute (with some quasi-democratic trimmings), and the state rested firmly for the time being on strong and disciplined military force. But the nation was subject to new stresses which manifested themselves in the various levels of intellectual stratification. Many accepted uncritically and even fanatically the nationalist doctrine, but numerous radical elements propagated socialism. The Social Democrat Party (founded and consolidated under other names in 1863 and 1875) survived the persecution of Bismarck and pursued the path pointed by Karl Marx (1818–83) under its present name from 1890; naturalistic literature displayed for the most part strong left-wing sympathies.

Yet it may be that the psychological theories proclaimed with dogmatic intransigence by the Viennese medical professor Sigmund Freud (1856–1939) effected a revolution in thought more fundamental and more far-reaching than that sought by the Marxists. In *Die Traumdeutung* (1900) and in *Drei Abhandlungen zur Sexualtheorie* (1905) Freud established the importance of the subconscious in the human mind, adding to thought a new dimension of depth and opening up new paths to playwrights and novelists. The insistence on Freudian orthodoxy should not, however, blind us to the important work of A. Adler (1870–1937) and especially C. G. Jung (1875–1961), which transcended the limitations of the strictly Freudian view.

2. *Expressionism: 1914–1933*

In retrospect the last decade of the nineteenth century and the first of the twentieth appear to have been a time of stability. The threat of social revolution so vividly aroused in 1871 by the Paris Commune had retreated and the German Empire apparently rested four-square on a formidable army, led by an efficient, aristocratic officer corps, and on an entrenched middle class which was in complete command of the field of education. The strength was real, but, as events were to show, it could be dissipated. When the prudence of Bismarck was replaced by the hectoring nationalism of William II stresses and cracks soon became apparent in international relationships in Europe. From 1905 on crisis followed crisis, as the military forces of Germany, France, Russia and Austria–Hungary were expanded and re-equipped, and the navies of Germany and Great Britain competed in building new and heavier battle squadrons. Eventually a climate prevailed in which war was desired by few but regarded by many as inevitable. Against this frightening manifestation of human impotence in face of a militant technology the voices of poets were raised here and there before the storm broke. The poems of Georg Heym (1887–1912) especially reflect the desolation of the great city and the brooding threat of war, the whole sultry atmosphere of the years immediately preceding the Great War.

Other voices too spoke out in question, protest or anguish. Reinhard Sorge (1892–1916), who was killed in the War, wrote one of the earliest expressionist plays, *Der Bettler* (1912), in which representation is abandoned and anonymous voices wrestle with the gap between generations and with the whole meaning of life. A similar generation problem infuses the disturbing play *Der Sohn* (1914) by W. Hasenclever (1890–1940). Georg Kaiser (1878–1945), after tentative beginnings, began in *Die Bürger von Calais* (1914, concerned with the episode linked with Edward III in 1347) a series of exclamatory and rhetorical plays, all preaching humanitarianism and some denouncing the encroachments of technology and the tyranny of the machine. They include *Von morgens bis mitternachts* (1916), the so-called *Gas* trilogy, composed of *Die Koralle* (1917), *Gas I* (1918) and *Gas II* (1920) and, late in life, *Das Floss der Medusa* (posth. 1963). Ernst Toller (1893–1939), whose life ended tragically in suicide, became a revolutionary Communist, and his incisive, disjointed plays are acts of protest with a strong individual imprint. *Masse-Mensch* (1921) sides with revolution yet laments the violence and suffering which accompany it, and *Die Maschinenstürmer* (1922)

111

dramatises the story of the English Luddites. *Feuer aus den Kesseln* (1930), a play of the fleet mutiny of 1918, is the tragedy of two political martyrs, and *Die blinde Göttin* (1932) concerns a wrongful conviction and its consequences.

The shrill emphasis of the expressionist dramatists is at its most strident in the early plays of Franz Werfel (1890–1945), notably in *Spiegelmensch* (1920); his later dramatic work, seen in *Juarez und Maximilian* (1924), *Das Reich Gottes in Böhmen* (1930) and his 'comedy of a tragedy' *Jacobowsky und der Oberst* (1944) is both more conventional and more powerful. From the mid–1920s Werfel, a highly intelligent critic of his time, expressed himself more successfully in novels. His sensitive fictional study of Verdi, *Verdi. Roman der Oper* (1924), has as its deliberate anti-climax a confrontation between Verdi and Wagner which never takes place because of Wagner's sudden death. His deep interest in Verdian opera led him to provide German opera houses with translations which both were singable and made sense. *Die Geschwister von Neapel* (1931), a novel of social transition, also has as one of its important motifs an operatic aria. Werfel had deep religious sympathies and, though a Jew, expressed in several novels affinities of feeling with the Roman Catholic Church, though he was never converted. These include *Barbara oder Die Frömmigkeit* (1929), *Der veruntreute Himmel* (1939) and *Das Lied von Bernardette* (1941). *Die vierzig Tage des Musa Dagh* (1933) expresses his sympathy with the persecuted, and his last novel *Stern der Ungeborenen* (1946) peers anxiously into the future. Ricarda Huch (1864–1947) deserves mention as an almost symbolical figure, born in the year of the first war of Prussian aggression in the nineteenth century, living through the monarchical, the republican and the National Socialist phase, courageously resisting the latter and surviving to witness its collapse. Her work moves through a border region of history and imagination, and the peaks of her achievement are not conventional historical novels but fictitious accounts of human life seen through the eyes of the historian, e.g. *Der grosse Krieg in Deutschland* (1912–14), which portrays the Thirty Years War, or *Michael Bakunin und die Anarchie* (1923).

Younger than Ricarda Huch and older than Werfel was the most original novelist of the twentieth century, Franz Kafka (1883–1924), whose work remained largely unknown, and indeed much of it unpublished, during his lifetime. As concise and fluent in his style as his contemporaries the Expressionists were blatant and incoherent, Kafka explored relentlessly the uncharted depths of his own soul, and his disturbing findings have held a later generation spell-bound. He is known to have been dominated by a strong-minded father and to have been oppressed by a deep sense of guilt. These facts colour his work, but they do not explain it. The least ostentatious of authors, he wrote because he felt driven to express himself, but displayed little interest in communication, even requesting that his substantial unpublished works should be destroyed after his death. This injunction was not observed. The quite literally nightmarish quality of Kafka's fiction has to be recognised if it is to be appreciated at all. Of the works published before his death, *Das Urteil* and *Die Verwandlung* (both 1916), have international repute. Both reflect the father complex. In *Das Urteil* guilt is admitted and sentence self-inflicted; in *Die Verwandlung* the imaginative metamorphosis of Gregor Samsa into an insect and its consequences are recounted with reticent but deeply felt compassion. Kafka's two posthumously published novels, *Der Prozess* (1925) and *Das Schloss* (1926, unfinished) are enigmatic, fascinating and beautifully written. The central figure in both is K., who is not to be interpreted as one and the same person, though an obvious allusion to Kafka himself is in each case intended. Both novels are baffling, but not wantonly so. Kafka is concerned with probing existence at a level at which he himself finds it baffling. In *Der Prozess* K. is, in the normal sense, utterly blameless, yet he appears to incur guilt, to which he himself admits, by the mere fact of his existence. The work includes the short parable *Vor dem Gesetz*, already published in Kafka's lifetime (1919). The remoteness and inaccessibility of the castle in *Das Schloss* is a parable of the difficulty of attaining certainty in important aspects of existence. In spite of the limpid clarity of Kafka's prose, the obscurity prevailing in the depths in which his mind moves has made of his work a happy hunting ground for interpreters of the most diverse convictions.

Profound and terrible though the effects of the First World War were on millions of fighting-men and their families, its direct results in literature were at first slender. There is no obvious German equivalent to Henri Barbusse's *Le Feu* (1916). The brave but sensitive regular officer Fritz von Unruh (1885–1970) tried to portray the horror and the suffering in the play *Vor der Entscheidung* and in the narrative of the tragic slaughter at Verdun *Opfergang*, but both were suppressed by the censorship until after the War (1919). In the immediate aftermath of war most writers turned their backs on the fighting and looked hopefully to the future. The work of Ernst Jünger (1895–), *In Stahlgewittern* (1920), stands alone as a fully realistic description of war, which is at the same time conceived in terms of austere and even mystical military devotion. When National Socialism came Jünger kept aloof and in 1939 published an anti-totalitarian parable, the story *Auf den Marmorklippen*.

One of the writers most influential on the intelligentsia of the younger generation after the war was Herman Hesse (1877–1962), who had spent the war years as a pacifist in Switzerland. His early novels *Peter Camenzind* (1904) and *Unterm Rad* (1906) had dealt with sensitive individuals at odds with a stereotyped, institutional society. The first has a conciliatory end, *Unterm Rad* is a tragedy. Hesse's first post-war novel, *Demian. Die Geschichte von Emil Sinclairs Jugend* (1919), revives the same theme with an element of mysticism, contrasting the man of independent spirit and depth of thought with the mindless herd. The implied condemnation of a world crumbling into ruin is repeated in *Der Steppenwolf* (1927), a bizarre and paradoxical novel, the hero of which is the 'lone wolf' Harry Haller. Up to this point Hesse's work combines a pronounced individualism and a youthful idealism with something of the *Kulturpessimismus* of Oswald Spengler (1889–1936), whose *Der Untergang des Abendlandes* (1918–22) was profoundly influential in the first post-war years. In Hesse's later works artistic, intellectual and spiritual values assert themselves. In *Narziss und Goldmund* (1930) a history

114

of unsatisfactory wayward exploration of the temporal and sensual culminates in reunciation and a sublimation of the relationship between the master Narziss and his pupil Goldmund. *Das Glasperlenspiel* (1943), widely read in Britain as *The Glass Bead Game*, is a remarkable Utopian novel which draws its mystical element from Christian and even more from oriental sources. Largely through these later works there has been a considerable revival in Hesse's standing in the 1960s and 1970s.

The once considerable influence of Stefan Zweig (1881–1942) has lapsed in recent years, possibly through the decline in interest in *biographies romancées* (so popular in the 1930s), of which Zweig wrote a number, dealing with such figures as Fouché, Marie Antoinette, Erasmus, Mary Queen of Scots and Magellan. Zweig was a perceptive critic of literature and art who in *Der Kampf mit dem Dämon* (1925) produced imaginative studies of Hölderlin, Heinrich von Kleist and Nietzsche. His *Novellen* (*Angst*, 1920, *Verwirrung der Gefühle*, 1922) reflect the intricacy and depth of the Viennese psycho-analytical approach.

Some ten years after the Great War ended there occurred an unexpected recrudescence of war experiences in literature, which rapidly proliferated. It began with the vivid war novel of a minor writer, Erich Maria Remarque (1898–1970), whose *Im Westen nichts Neues* (1929), portraying the sufferings of the front-line soldier with crass realism and deep compassion, created an immediate and wide impression, evoking enthusiasm from the liberally-minded and fury from the nationalists. Curiously enough, it was preceded by two notable war novels, *Der Streit um den Sergeanten Grischa* (1926) by Arnold Zweig (1887–1968) and *Krieg* (1928) by the Communist aristocrat Ludwig Renn (1889– , real name Arnold Vieth von Golssenau), both works of high quality which yet failed to provoke the furore which followed *Im Westen nichts Neues*. A spate of war novels followed in the early 1930s, many of which, in sharp contrast to Remarque's book, were glorifications of war.

However, the war did not take over literature entirely. Contemporaneous with *Im Westen nichts Neues* was the novel *Berlin Alexanderplatz* (1929) by Alfred Döblin (1878–1957), a

Social Democrat doctor working among the poor. *Berlin Alexanderplatz* is the story of a criminal who, in spite of genuine efforts to go straight, is dragged down again into criminality. But the work is remarkable, less for its plot, than for the extraordinary success with which Döblin captures the confusing complex character of the quarter of the great city which provides the setting. The originality of his language is astonishing; the most cavalier disregard of syntax, reinforced by abundant colloquial expressions and by current slang, results in great vitality and pungency. *Berlin Alexanderplatz*, somewhat unfairly, has overshadowed Döblin's later novels, which include *Pardon wird nicht gegeben* (1935), the four volumes of *November 1918* (1939–50), and *Hamlet oder Die lange Nacht nimmt ein Ende* (1956).

Other writers of Döblin's generation held public attention also for a time after 1945. Ernst Wiechert (1887–1950) wrote East Prussian novels such as *Die Magd des Jürgen Doskocil* (1932), and after the War published *Die Jerominkinder* (1945–7), a long chronicle, the closing stages of which are anti-National Socialist, and *Missa sine nomine* (1950), a rather emotional treatment of the aftermath of Nazism. He owed his temporary prominence rather more to his graphic and horrifying account of his confinement in 1938 in a concentration camp (*Der Totenwald*, 1945). In *Der Grosstyrann und das Gericht* (1935) Werner Bergengruen (1892–1964) grappled courageously with the problem of authoritarianism, incorporating it in a kind of Renaissance detective story. His nostalgic post-war work (e.g. *Der letzte Rittmeister*, 1952) had only a limited appeal. Ina Seidel (1885–1974), a novelist of a strong Protestant tradition, wrote two solid and deeply compassionate novels, *Das Labyrinth* (1922, dealing with Georg(e) Forster, who voyaged with Captain Cook) and *Das Wunschkind* (1930, set at the time of the Napoleonic Wars). Her post-war novels (including *Das unverwesliche Erbe*, 1954, and *Michaela*, 1959) have an air of apologia. A more considerable and somewhat underrated writer is the Catholic convert Gertrud von le Fort (1876–1971), who wrote excellent historical *Novellen* (*Die Letzte am Schafott*, 1931, *Am Tor des Himmels*, 1954), and also contributed two novels of outstanding quality, *Das*

116

Schweisstuch der Veronika, which appeared in two widely separated volumes (1928 and 1946) and the impressive and deeply moving historical novel *Die magdeburgische Hochzeit* (1938, dealing with the events surrounding the sack of Magdeburg in 1631).

Carl Zuckmayer (1896–) may properly be mentioned here, for though his two outstanding successes are closer to naturalism than to the movements which followed, his message was addressed to a later generation. *Der Hauptmann von Köpenick* (1930), based on a true incident, is a brilliant comedy on the theme of appearance and reality and a satire on militarism. *Des Teufels General* (1946, originating in the career of the air force General Udet) is both a graphic picture of National Socialist Berlin in the War and a serious discussion of the ethics of guilt and responsibility. So convincing is the rendering that it is difficult to realise that it is an imaginary reconstruction written in neutral Switzerland. The play *Das kalte Licht* (1955), which has as its theme the betrayal of secret atomic research, enjoyed a success primarily because its subject was topical.

Of the generation writing between the two wars and immediately after the second, two Marxists remain to be mentioned. The lyric poet Gottfried Benn (1886–1956) began with protest against the conditions of existence. After this initial phase of expressionist poetry he became less and less a programmatic poet and more and more an experimenter with vocabulary and syntax. The poems of this trend are contained in the collections *Fragmente* (1951), *Destillationen* (1953) and *Aprèslude* (1955). Though Benn's name is now less frequently heard than ten years ago, there is no doubt that the precision, coolness and originality of his language powerfully influenced younger German poets in the 1950s.

The other Marxist has achieved world-wide fame. Even after the revival of Hermann Hesse and the advent of Böll and Grass, Bert Brecht (1898–1956) remains, with Thomas Mann, the modern German author most familiar to English readers. A frankly committed writer, Brecht sought to revolutionise the theatre, turning it in to a pulpit for Socialism, and his theory of detachment or alienation (*Verfremdungseffekt*) is designed

117

to throw his collective message into a clear and unfamiliar light and so to prevent its being obscured by sympathy with the suffering individual. Yet his intention is not infrequently thwarted by his power to people his 'epic theatre' with sentient, credible human beings who engage our lively interest in spite of the author; of this Mother Courage in the play *Mutter Courage und ihre Kinder* (1941) is perhaps the most conspicuous example. From the early *Trommeln in der Nacht* (1922), through *Die Dreigroschenoper* (1928), *Aufstieg und Fall der Stadt Mahagonny* (1930), *Das Leben des Galilei* (1943), *Der gute Mensch von Sezuan* (1943) to *Der kaukasische Kreidekreis* (not forgetting *Mutter Courage* already mentioned) Brecht has written a mass of plays which, by virtue of their vigour, transparence and translatability, have had access to theatres all over the world and have notably enriched the dramatic repertoire.[1]

3. The Second World War and After

The German monarchy, which came to an end with the departure of the Emperor William II in 1918, was succeeded by the so-called Weimar Republic. The uneasy history of this state, which had few friends at home and fewer abroad, was terminated in 1933 by the paradoxical appointment by the monarchistic President Hindenburg of Hitler, a fanatical demagogue, to be Chancellor of the realm. The Weimar Republic had been a time of licence and experiment for literature. With the coming of National Socialism nearly all the independent writers either emigrated or fell silent. The Aryan racialists, the patriotic nationalists and the earth-bound regionalists (*Heimatkünstler*) had the field to themselves.

The total collapse of 1945 with all the destruction and terrible loss of life in the homeland (which Germany had escaped in the First World War) was all the more shattering for its contrast to and its connection with the brash self-confidence which had prevailed in 1939 and 1940. A new, hitherto unheard and deeply disillusioned generation began to write with

[1] The dates are those of the first performance in German.

a new freedom and in new tones. The voices of the well-known emigrants, such as Thomas Mann, had little to say to the newcomers. But, as always, there were forerunners, men neglected in their own day, whose works were either now published for the first time or recalled from obscurity. Four or five figures born in the nineteenth century slowly crept to prominence as men who had anticipated the problems of the new world of 1945 and after, or whose style was free from the inflation which had characterised much German writing for more than a century. The first to achieve eminence was no longer there to enjoy or despise it. Robert Musil (1880–1942) wrote very little, and what he did write was scarcely noticed until after 1945. His subtle and distressing short novel *Die Verwirrungen des Zöglings Törless* (1906) is an important literary contribution to the psychology of adolescence and has been turned into a successful film. His most important work, the very long novel *Der Mann ohne Eigenschaften* (three volumes published respectively in 1930, 1933 and 1943, issued, so far as possible, complete in 1965) remorselessly and with razor-sharp intelligence examines human action and motive and gives to his characters a background in which the qualities and fallibilities of Austria–Hungary are analysed with profound penetration and irresistible irony. But the vision extends wider than 'Kakanien', as he calls his native country, to comprehend the *malaise* of the whole civilised world and to question its accepted values. Robert Walser (1878–1956), a Swiss, whose writing ceased in 1933, was not 'discovered' until about 1960. His novel *Jakob von Gunten* (1909) deals disturbingly with adolescent problems, and his short stories and sketches (collected as *Dichtungen in Prosa*, 1953–62) explore, with detached irony and a curious self-effacing withdrawal, problems of existence similar to those probed by Kafka. Hermann Broch (1886–1951) gave up industry for literature at the age of forty-two. He emigrated to the United States in 1938, studied politics and became a professor at Yale. Broch's two best-known novels have a mystical visionary character. *Der Tod des Vergil* (1945) presents Virgil's thoughts in the form of an interior monologue as death approaches, questioning human values and finally affirming the validity of *caritas*. What Broch called his *Bergroman* is political, studying the behaviour and psychology of the masses in a time of degeneration. It is unfinished and was first published in 1953 under the descriptive but incorrect title *Der Versucher*. Broch's third draft appeared in 1967 as *Demeter* (a title which he had contemplated) and all three drafts were published together in 1968 under his own workaday heading *Bergroman*. The complexity and obscurity of Broch's writing makes his work somewhat inaccessible, but the effort to overcome the difficulties brings rewards. Another solitary, Hans Henny Jahnn (1894–1959), an eccentric North German organ-maker, took refuge on Bornholm, returning to Germany in 1950. From his early plays (*Pastor Ephraim Magnus*, 1919, and *Neuer Lübecker Totentanz*, 1931) to his postwar trilogy *Fluss ohne Ufer* (1949–61) his work is concerned with a revaluation of civilisation, an exaltation of the senses and the flesh, and an anarchic reaction against the rule of reason. The Austrian Heimito von Doderer (1896–1966) wrote several barely noticed novels between 1930 and 1950. In 1951 *Die Strudlhofstiege* made him famous overnight. Obviously written with great art, the novel purports not to select, but to render 'all' – to be 'der totale Roman'. It is peopled by a host of figures, whose characters are analysed with distinction and insight, and Doderer has managed to intertwine them successfully and yet not artificially, and to portray with meticulous detail and evocative atmosphere the topography of the districts of Vienna in which they live. This novel was followed by *Die Dämonen* (to which it is a prelude) in 1926; it is a vast and detailed work constructed on similar lines and having for its centre-piece the burning down of the Palace of Justice in Vienna by a rioting mob on 15 July 1927. Doderer's ambition extended to a much more comprehensive work chronicling, in four separate novels, life in Vienna from 1880 to 1960. The first appeared as *Roman Nr. 7. Die Wasserfälle von Slunj* in 1963; the rest remained uncompleted, but a fragment of the second volume was published in 1967 as *Der Grenzwald*.

The generation which was in its twenties when Hitler came to power and served in the War when thirty or more has produced some competent and for the most part unsensational writing. Stefan Andres (1906–70) was the author of sensitive

novels such as *Die Hochzeit der Feinde* (1947) and oi
Novelle, Wir sind Utopia, a story of the Spanish Civil War
which the political problem is illuminated with an intense
spirituality. Between 1949 and 1959 he produced an ambitious
trilogy of politico-philosophical novels, *Die Sintflut*. Albrecht
Goes (1908–   ), a pastor's son and a Christian theologian, is
chiefly known for the *Novelle, Das Brandopfer* (1945), a story
of moral responsibility and human compassion against a background of the war-time persecution of the Jews. A more remote event, the compulsory withdrawal of the Jesuits in 1769
from the ideal state they had set up in Paraguay, is exploited
by Fritz Hochwälder (1911–   ) in *Das heilige Experiment*
(1947), a play in which idealism is crushed by a hostile prag-
matic world.

During the Second World War Switzerland was a kind of
neutral observation post, the occupiers of which uneasily contemplated the warring world around them. From this safe but
discomforting situation there emerged after the War two
writers who quickly gained a European reputation and
considerable influence upon Germany itself. Max Frisch
(1911–   ) has written a series of plays, of which the first (*Nun
singen sie wieder*, 1946) is a commemoration of the dead, the
second (*Die chinesische Mauer*, 1947) a parable of the threat
of nuclear warfare, and the others (*Biedermann und die
Brandstifter*, 1956, and *Andorra*, 1958) warnings of what has
been and could be again. All deserve the term parable, and
techniques of black comedy, satire and surrealism are frequently used. While writing these plays Frisch has also become deeply interested in the problem of identity, which is the
subject of the novels *Stiller* (1954) and *Mein Namen sei Gan-
tenbein* (1964) and of the play *Graf Öderland* (1951, revised
1961). Human weakness and vulnerability is with Frisch
closely associated with identity. He regards his diaries, *Tagebuch 1946–49* (1950) and *Tagebuch 1966–71* (1972) as an important part of his oeuvre. Friedrich Dürrenmatt (1921–   )
has criticised the world in which he grew up and which persists in disregarding the warnings of the past, in a series of
grotesque comedies of serious intent. They begin with *Es
steht geschrieben* (1947) and *Der Blinde* (1948), which may

be called historical tragi-comedies, continue with the black comedies *Romulus der Grosse* (1949) and *Die Ehe des Herrn Mississippi* (1952), and reach their highest level in *Der Besuch der alten Dame* (1956) and *Die Physiker* (1962). Mention should also be made of the grotesque *Frank der Fünfte. Oper einer Privatbank* (1960), the comedy of death *Der Meteor* (1966) and the bleak quasi-apocalyptic *Porträt eines Planeten* (1971). Dürrenmatt is also widely known in Britain for his short and entertaining detective novels, which are largely pre-occupied with serious ideas of guilt and retribution (*Der Richter und sein Henker*, 1951, *Der Verdacht*, 1952, and *Das Versprechen*, 1958).

Among the writers of the so-called 'Inner Emigration', those who wrote little or nothing in the Hitler years but remained in Germany, were Hermann Kasack (1896–1966), Heinz Risse (1898–), Wolfgang Koeppen (1906–) and Gerd Gaiser (1908–), each of whom produced a remarkable novel in the early post-war years. Kasack's *Die Stadt hinter dem Strom* (1947) exhibits in surrealist terms a ghostly transition from robust normal life on one side of the river to a land of ruin, desolation and death on the other, and in doing so provides a striking record of the mental as well as the physical state of that time of death-like devastation. Heinz Risse's *Wenn die Erde bebt* (1950) uses an earthquake as symbol of the catastrophe, and pessimistically contemplates the ants (symbols of humanity) busily reconstructing exactly what has been destroyed. An equally critical view of the new society of the post-war years emerges in the novels of Wilhelm Koeppen, published between 1951 and 1954 in a spurt of activity which is the more remarkable in that he has written no novel since. *Tauben im Gras* (1951) deals critically with the problems of the new Federal Republic at the time of the currency reform; *Das Treibhaus* (1953), set at the advent of the 'Economic Miracle' – the hot-house of the title is the political world of Bonn – portrays a politician who has no faith in the policies he supports. *Der Tod im Rom* (1954) carries the cynicism further, showing the rise of corruption and the trend of former National Socialists to insinuate themselves into high positions in politics and administration. Gerd Gaiser (1908–), a pastor's son and former fighter pilot, treated the theme of the returning soldier in *Eine Stimme hebt an* (1950), relived the German airman's experience of forlorn endeavour in *Die Sterbende Jagd* (1953) and in *Schlussball* (1958) used a highly original technique to present a devastating analysis of contemporary German society, so adding his voice to that of Koeppen. Luise Rinser (1911–   ), a Roman Catholic, was condemned to death in 1945 and saved by the Allied victory. She published in 1946 her moving *Gefängnis-Tagebuch*. Her inter-related novels *Mitte des Lebens* (1950) and *Abenteuer der Tugend* (1957) were published as a single work, *Nina*, in 1961. Her themes revolve largely round women and children, but she is also acutely aware of the general crisis of the age, as the novel *Wie, wenn wir ärmer würden oder Die Heimkehr des verlorenen Sohnes* (1974) shows.

The principal East German novelists of this time are Anna Seghers (1900–   ) and Erwin Strittmatter (1912–   ). Both conform with the somewhat restrictive literary policy of the government without apparent discomfort. The prescribed social realism does not deprive their works of merit, and Strittmatter, whose writing has been entirely under the GDR, has published the novels *Ochsenkutscher* (1950), *Tinko* (1954), and *Der Wundertäter* (1957); he has also composed in *Katzgraben* (1954) an excellent verse comedy. Anna Seghers was a Communist well before 1933 and it is noticeable that her best works – the *Novelle, Der Aufstand der Fischer von St. Barbara* (1928), and the novels *Das siebte Kreuz* (1942), *Transit* (1944) and *Die Toten bleiben jung* (1947) – belong, except for the last, to her time of opposition. Though the later novels do not maintain this level, the writing retains vitality and her commitment to social justice is obvious.

The young men who were boys when Hitler came to power had as their first experience of manhood the inhuman shams of the Nazi regime and the hardships and horrors of war. Virtually the first literary impact after the war was made by Wolfgang Borchert (1921–47), whose caustic utterances while serving as a soldier led to terms of imprisonment. With an ironical technique which has affinities with expressionism Borchert portrayed in *Draussen vor der Tür* (performed both

Hamburg Radio and in the theatre in 1947) the situation of the soldier returning homeless and lonely to a country in ruins. He was thus the first to touch the theme of the *Heimkehrer*, which was to recur in so many variations in the next few years.

It was in 1947 also that two journalists, one of whom was Alfred Andersch (1914–), founded a left-wing periodical in Munich, which the U.S. authorities banned. This incident led to a meeting attended by various writers, out of which arose the Gruppe 47. This group was little more than a fluctuating association without official membership; its one event was an annual conference at which work was read and criticised. Among those who attended at various times were, apart from Andersch, H. Böll, Ingeborg Bachmann, G. Eich, M. Walser, H. M. Enzensberger, G. Grass, S. Lenz and U. Johnson. After a very few years its influence declined, but it lingered on until 1967. It encouraged new attitudes to and techniques of writing and was a manifestation of the same desire for a new start indicated by the word *Kahlschlag* (clearance) adopted by W. Weyrauch (1907–) in 1949.

Andersch himself wrote little of note, but the story *Sansibar oder der letzte Grund* (1957) was widely read and the novel *Winterspelt* (1974) also attracted attention. From 1958 Andersch lived abroad, dissatisfied with both Germanies, West and East. Among those whose names were much associated with the Gruppe 47 in the early days was Heinrich Böll (1917–), whose early fiction is linked with his war experiences. The short novel *Der Zug war pünklich* (1949) was followed by *Wanderer, kommst du nach Spa?* (1950, containing stories concerned with the aftermath as well as with war itself), and then by the cycle *'Wo warst du, Adam?'* (1951), stories which are linked more or less loosely by the figure of the soldier Feinhals. The answer to God's question from Genesis is 'Ich war im Weltkrieg'. Böll's world of war is not the epic of mud, sweat, shell-holes and deafening barrages which in the novels of between the wars generated, largely unintentionally, a legend of heroism. His vision, for all its sympathy, is unwaveringly ironic, and war with all its horrors is a succession of absurdities. In the mid-1950s Böll wrote a group of three

124

short novels dealing with the social problems of the chaotic Germany of the immediate post-war years. *Und sagte kein einziges Wort* (1953) and *Hause ohne Hüter* (1954), though not lacking in compassion, are critical and ironic. *Das Brot der frühen Jahre* (1955) is more positive and encouraging. A man in whose make-up conscience and the sense of justice play a prominent part, Böll became in his middle years one of the principal 'dissenters' in the Federal Republic. The novel *Billard um halb zehn* (1959) is still primarily retrospective. The later novels employ ingenious techniques to take the callous, affluent and materialistic society to task (*Ansichten eines Clowns*, 1963, *Ende einer Dienstfahrt*, 1966, *Gruppenbild mit Dame*, 1971, and *Die verlorene Ehre der Katharina Blüm*, 1974). His, largely political, essays, speeches, etc. were published as *Aufsätze, Kritiken, Reden* (1967).

The sensation of the 1960s was the irruption into literature of the strident boisterous personality of Günter Grass (1927–), whose novel *Die Blechtrommel* (1959) is almost as well known in Britain and America as it is in Germany. It is set in Danzig and seems to evoke every street in the city and every area in the surrounding countryside. By turns scurrilous, poetic and grotesque, it has as its 'hero' the dwarf Oskar Mazerath, a true *enfant terrible*, who intervenes and withdraws at will from the world around him, and accompanies his actions with a ruthless and penetrating political and social commentary. *Katz und Maus* (1961) is a shorter variation on a similar theme. The novel *Hundejahre* (1963) is equally evocative of the Danzig scene (Grass styled the three works *Danziger Trilogie*) and ranges ironically and provocatively from the war to the activities of former National Socialists in Germany. Grass's later novels *örtlich betäubt* (1969) and *Aus dem Tagebuch einer Schnecke* (1972) are less strident, but just as fascinating in technique and as clear in their social commitment.

Martin Walser (1927–) wrote novels containing caustic criticisms of contemporary West German society, some of which show a turn for erotic fantasy. They include *Ehen in Philippsburg* (1957) and the group of three centred on Anselm Kristlein: *Halbzeit* (1960), *Das Einhorn* (1966) and *Der Sturz* (1973). The ironic comedy *Eiche und Angora* (1962) satirises the successful survivors of the National Socialist regime. The writings of Siegfried Lenz (1926–) are also much concerned with conscience, but their tone is less bitter. The criticism is most obvious in the early novel *Duell mit dem Schatten* (1953), in the later long work *Deutschstunde* (1968) and in the play *Zeit der Schuldlosen* (1961). In lighter vein the stories in *So zärtlich war Suleyken* (1955) and *So war es mit dem Zirkus* (1971) conjure up his native Masuria. His experience of the sea, acquired during war service, underlies *Das Feuerschiff* (1960) and *Stimmungen der See* (1962).

The most original novelist of recent years in Germany is Uwe Johnson (1934–), who migrated to the West after his first novel was banned in East Germany. His best work so far is probably his second novel, *Mutmassungen über Jakob* (1959, the first remained unpublished), which begins with the death of a railwayman in fog and then, probing into a metaphorical fog of suppositions, gradually assembles a set of probabilities which can never attain certainty. This novel, like its two successors (*Das dritte Buch über Achim*, 1961, and *Zwei Ansichten*, 1965) is deeply concerned with the division of Germany and also with varying interpretations of Communism. Johnson's latest novel, *Jahrestage der Gesine Cresspahl*, is a brilliant feat of experimental narration evoking both present-day America and the history of Germany over the last forty years, largely by montage and flashback, but Johnson, having published the first three enormous volumes (1970–3), of what is intended to represent a kind of diary (or at least *diarium*) spanning a single year (August 1967–August 1968), seems uncertain whether or not to bring the work, which has tended to outgrow itself, to a conclusion with a fourth.

Like Martin Walser, Heinar Kipphardt (1922–) has written plays as well as fiction, and it happens that one of his best-known plays, *Der Hund des Generals* (1962), is an adaptation of one of his best-known stories bearing the same title (1957). It treats war satirically, making use of black humour. Kipphardt is also the author of documentary plays which have been televised (*In der Sache J. Robert Oppenheimer*, 1964, and *Joel Brand. Die Geschichte eines Geschäfts*, 1965). The technique of documentary montage for the stage has been most brilliantly developed by Peter Weiss (1916–) in *Die Ermittlung* (1965). Both this work and its predecessor *Die Verfolgung und Ermordung Jean Paul Marats, dargestellt durch die Schauspielgruppe des Hospizes zu Charenton unter Anleitung des Herrn de Sade* (1964), usually abbreviated to *Marat-Sade*, achieved European success. Rolf Hochhuth has been for some years the stormy petrel of the German theatre. The plays *Der Stellvertreter* (1963), dealing with the moral role and standing of the Pope in his relations with National Socialist Jewish policy, and *Soldaten* (1967), which claims that Churchill engineered General Sikorski's death, caused a furore of controversy; they purport to be based on documentary evidence which has not been disclosed. Hochhuth took the noteworthy step in these plays of reviving verse. He has continued to be a focus for controversy, though the later plays, *Guerrillas* (1970) and *Lysistrata und NATO* (1974) have been less sensational. Hochhuth's *Tod eines Jägers* (1976) is a monologue based on the death of Ernest Hemingway. The other dramatist of note in recent years is Peter Hacks (1928–), who migrated from West to East Germany in 1955. He has made his name with a number of historical plays conceived from a Marxist angle, which include *Die Schlacht bei Lobositz* (1956) and *Der Müller von Sanssouci* (1958), and with the verse comedy *Amphitryon* (1968). Sensation and even notoriety has been achieved by Peter Handke (1942–), whose play, which some may call an anti-play, *Der Ritt über den Bodensee* (1971) was stormily received; his *Publikumsbeschimpfung und andere Sprechstücke* (1966) had already expressed an intentionally cavalier attitude to the reader or spectator. For many, Handke's most impressive work is the story *Die Angst des Tormanns beim Elfmeter* (1970), in which an extended metaphor drawn from football is used in order to view an act of murder and the murderer's flight in a novel perspective.

I have left lyric poetry till last principally because poets, writing – if they are good poets – because they must, are not so easily classified under rubrics of fashion, though they are admittedly not without influence upon one another. Not that novelists and dramatists do not write from compulsion, but being professionals who live by their efforts, they heed fashion as well as helping to make it. Poets, partly because poetry *can* be an incidental activity, are numerous, and only a limited selection of the outstanding can be mentioned here.

Poets sometimes come to fame late, and Wilhelm Lehmann (1882–1968) is an example of one who lived to see it happen. His early novels are virtually forgotten, and the poems of *Antwort des Schweigens* (1935) met with little response. Now no anthology of modern verse is complete without several examples of his sensitive nature-poetry, contained in collections from *Der grüne Gott* (1942) on. Another late arrival was Marie Luise Kaschnitz (1901–74), whose moving lament 'Rückkehr nach Frankfurt' belongs to 1947. A religious poet, she does not brush difficulties aside, facing destruction and disintegration in disciplined and measured verse. Her collections include *Zukunftsmusik* (1950), *Dein Schweigen – meine Stimme* (1962) and *Ein Wort weiter* (1965). In her later years she also experimented with prose (e.g. *Beschreibung eines Dorfes*, 1966, among other works). Nelly Sachs (1891–1970), who herself narrowly escaped the fate of so many Jews in 1939–45, spoke as the living voice of the friendless, persecuted and massacred. Her poetry, as distinguished as it is compassionate, appeared in collections from *In den Wohnungen des Todes* (1947) to the posthumous *Teile dich Nacht* (1971). The other great poet who touched this theme is Paul Celan (1920–70), whose 'Todesfuge' is one of the great poems of the twentieth century; almost as deeply moving are the shorter 'Tenebrae' and 'Psalm'.

The revolution in the use of words in poetry begun by Gottfried Benn (and perhaps less obviously by Brecht) is already perceptible in the work of Marie Luise Kaschnitz and Nelly Sachs, and is prominent in the poetry of Paul Celan. Günter Eich (1907–72) carries it much further. A poet of *Kahlschlag*, seeking a clean sweep, he has provided the model of simple austerity and sparse economy in the constantly quoted poem 'Inventur'. Ingeborg Bachmann (1926–73) aroused great expectations with her first volumes of verse which contained the poems 'Grosse Landschaft bei Wien' (1953) and 'Anrufung des grossen Bären' (1956). The East German Peter Huchel (1903–   ) produced his finest work in the immediate post-war years with poems such as 'Chausseen' and 'Bericht eines Pfarrers vom Untergang seiner Gemeinde'. Johannes Bobrowski (1917–65) retained a vivid recollection of his homeland by the Memel, which he expressed in melancholy poems evoking both details of the landscape and the people who inhabited it, 'Sarmatische Zeit' (1961) and 'Schattenland Ströme' (1962). Endowed with an exceptional gift for memorable phrases, evident in 'Pruzzische Elegie' or 'Kindheit', he could also write powerful concentrated poems of terse understatement such as 'Bericht'.

During the 1950s and 1960s a development took place in poetry which was equivalent to the long-established practice of abstract art. Incomplete sentences, sentences without meaning, groups of words with no apparent connection were all used. Poems were composed as montage out of fragments abstracted or quoted from unrelated sources. A leading figure in this kind of poetry, which seeks a complete break with the past, is Helmut Heissenbüttel (1921–   ) with his series of *Textbücher* (annually 1960–7). A school of 'concrete poetry', led by E. Gomringer (1925–   ), arranges words in geometrical and other patterns employing various type-faces (*konstellationen*, 1953). Though serious criticism has been offered on these experiments, it is clear that playfulness is an important element. The possibility of introducing colour into *konkrete Dichtung* appears not yet to have been explored. A further variation of this type of poetry is the onomatopoeicism of Ernst Jandl (1925–   ), whose nonsense poems, which appear to be arbitrary collections of letters (*Lautgedichte*) yet produce a striking impression when read – especially by the author. Jandl is fortunately endowed with a gift of humour. Whether concrete poetry will lead to something even more esoteric, or produce a new popular movement, or simply fade away, is an undecided question.

Bibliographical Note

Whoever wishes to go further with German literature will have some idea about which authors he wishes to read first. Editions of complete writings, of selections and of single works are numerous and easily obtained. Translations of most modern and many older works are available. The list below mentions some works of reference which provide information on this and on the enormous field of books about German literature dealing with broad periods or specific writers.

Bibliographies are contained in the following histories of literature in English:

Introductions to German Literature, ed. A. Closs, 4 vols (Cresset, London, 1967–9).
A History of German Literature, J. G. Robertson (Blackwood, Edinburgh, 5th ed. 1966).

English translations of German works are listed in:

Cassell's Encyclopaedia of World Literature, 3 vols (London, 2nd ed. 1973).

The advanced student who wishes to go to German sources may advantageously consult:

Bibliographisches Handbuch des deutschen Schrifttums, J. Körner (Francke, Berne, 1949).
Einführung in die Bücherkunde zur deutschen Literaturwissenschaft, P. Raabe (Sammlung Metzler, Stuttgart, 1961).
Bücherkunde für Germanisten, J. Hansel (E. Schmidt-Verlag, Berlin, 1961).

Personalbibliographie zur deutschen Literaturgeschichte, J.
Hansel (E. Schmidt-Verlag, Berlin, 1967).
Also the numerous paper-back volumes of the Sammlung
Metzler (Stuttgart).

Anyone wishing only for basic information from a German
source will find it in:

Deutsches Dichterlexikon, G. von Wilpert (Kröner, Stuttgart, 1963)
and
Sachwörterbuch zur deutschen Literatur, G. von Wilpert
(Kröner, Stuttgart, 4th ed. 1964).

Biographies of authors, synopses of their works and related
matters are given in *The Oxford Companion to German
Literature*, H. and M. Garland (Clarendon Press, Oxford,
1976).
A German dictionary of contemporary authors only is:
A. Endres, *Autorenlexikon der deutschen Gegenwart* (1975).

Index

Index